·WASHINGTON HOSTESS COOKBOOK·

Designed by Philip Clucas
Photography by Neil Sutherland
Contributing Editor Cissie Coy
Edited by Jane Adams and Jillian Stewart
Stylist Hanni Penrose

CLB 2152

This 1990 edition published by Portland House, a division of dilithium Press, Ltd.
Distributed by Crown Publishers, Inc. 225 Park Avenue South, New York, New York 10003.
Printed and bound in Hong Kong.

ISBN 0 517 65875 5
h g f e d c b a

·WASHINGTON HOSTESS COOKBOOK·

·CISSIE COY·

PORTLAND HOUSE

National Symphony Orchestra

· Washington Hostess Cookbook ·

· CONTENTS ·

·Washington Hostess Cookbook·

·INTRODUCTION·

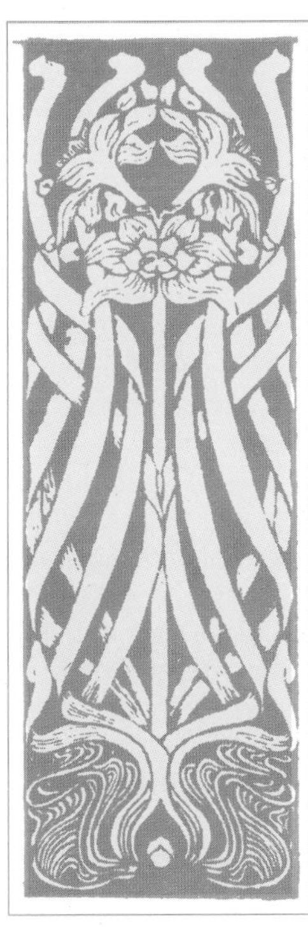

The capital of the Great Republic gathered its people from the four winds of heaven, and so the manners, the faces and the fashions there, presented a variety that was infinite.
Mark Twain

This book invites you into the private world of a most public city. It draws back the curtain to offer glimpses of fifteen Washington hostesses entertaining in their homes as they do for friends. And because the line between business and pleasure often blurs in the Capital, you will see both "official" and unofficial Washington preparing to have a good time. These are not the picture postcard scenes of white marble landmarks. Instead, these are the drawing rooms and dining rooms where the power people and their neighbors relax.

The public city that is Washington, D.C. is incomparable. Frenchman Pierre L'Enfant's visionary plan is realized in wide swaths of green parks, broad avenues, flower-banked promenades, and the monuments that are symbols of democracy.

Lady Bird Johnson, wife of President Lyndon Johnson, left a lasting floral legacy; her Beautification Campaign of the 1960s still blossoms across the United States and especially in Washington. The National Park Service keeps the the landscape ablaze with rainbow displays, moving from fall chrysanthemums to midsummer geraniums, heliotrope and roses. With the exception of the FBI building which is a sore thumb, Pennsylvania Avenue, the ceremonial spine of Washington, is lined with handsome and historic buildings like the Beaux Arts restored Willard Hotel (where Lincoln and other presidents awaited their inauguration).

There are well-publicized problems here as there are in any big city, but tourism continues to be the second largest source of revenue. Twenty million tourists a year wait through rain and shine to tour the White House, pass through metal detectors to view Congress in action, and drive at a snail's pace around the Tidal Basin in the spring to catch the extravaganza of pink cherry blossoms. Occasionally, not often, they even catch a glimpse of the presidential entourage speeding around a corner or pass a congressman holding a press conference on the West Front of the Capitol.

Even without that glimpse or chance encounter, there is the thrill of witnessing living history. When you move through the White House East Room, you remember that Thomas Jefferson walked there. In the Senate Chamber, you look down on the desks where legislative giants debate issues that affect your freedom. The Smithsonian's Air and Space Museum, the most popular museum on the Mall, hangs Lindbergh's tiny *Spirit of Saint Louis* over a space capsule.

That is Washington's public face.

Behind the imposing facades, behind the clichés about politicians and occasional scandals, are 3.7 million people from the metropolitan area who work and play here. People who make up the "real" Washington. The business people. And, there's only one business in town – government. Everything else radiates out from government, so the interlocking circles of people in Washington are constantly changing but never get too far away from the center.

Power conveys instant social status. And, though it is increasingly difficult, power is obtainable without a personal fortune. Work is the talk, substance and currency of Washington, and all too often what you do is who you are. On the other hand, the town has accepted chiefs of state whose résumés list everything from military experience, to peanut farming and acting. Washingtonians have to be, at the least, flexible.

In the interlocking circles surrounding the politically powerful of government are media people, lobbyists, consultants, lawyers, and diplomats. The supporting cast includes "cave dwellers" (wealthy descendants of the earliest settlers), real estate agents, caterers, university faculty, builders, shop owners, plumbers. They are all part of the "real" Washington.

Not a few social critics contend that Washingtonians take themselves too seriously. Certainly some do. The elixir of power and prominence is a heady draught, often lethal: the obsession for getting power, keeping it, being near it. But all generalities have exceptions and there are lots of exceptions. Alta Leath, wife of a Texas congressman, puts it simply, "If you come here mature, you get your feet on the ground in a hurry. I don't think Washington's competitive."

What few people see, obviously, is the private life of real Washingtonians. What really goes on when the draperies are pulled closed and candles soften the lines on famous faces? The circles bump up against one another in the social whirl and the resulting electricity is fascinating. The machinery of government is oiled over cocktails and canapes. Insiders know the importance of Washington's social interactions – the phone lines are hot the morning after a great party!

Entertaining at home, as Washingtonians do, reveals the personality of the hostess as clearly as a Rorschach test! She can be described by the collections she treasures, the individuality of the decorations she chooses, even the way she manages the inevitable crisis – and these hostesses have those, too. Not every setting is grand and not every meal elaborate. Food can be as competitive as politics, but a good party doesn't mean intimidating, pretentious menus. Anything goes. Grace Nelson enjoys giving busy friends a chance to get to know one another's children by giving mother-daughter teas. Jayne Ikard says that she'll never forget a distinguished ambassador guest asking his wife why they never served black beans with rice at *their* house. Carol Lascaris and her husband are a cooking team, preparing the Greek food he saw his mother and grandmother cooking; what her great-uncle, she laughs, would call "wet food." Esther Coopersmith mixes the cabinet, congress and diplomatic world and serious conversation over a casual barbecue. Gail Berendzen is wife of American University's President Richard Berendzen; when she serves a buffet breakfast for honor students and student leaders, she wants it to be substantial enough to send them off to a good day of classes.

Be a guest behind scenes. You'll find that there are many ways of entertaining and that each ultimately succeeds not because of a grand staff or a fleet of caterers, but because of the thought, effort and caring of the hostess. These women sit around board tables, card tables and dinner tables with equal poise. They give a new slant to the word "hostess" that takes it out of the salon and brings it into the twenty-first century.

The stereotype "hostess" perpetuates an image of a frivolous woman whose invitations were taken seriously while she herself was not. She gave six-course dinners with gold service plates and there was a three to one ratio, guests to butler. This woman was specially bred to the art of entertainment and she had the house, staff, and leisure to maintain a proper salon. Women like her rarely worked outside the home, and this was the only access she had to influence and power.

In fact, Washington's last "hostess" was not frivolous and she is well remembered in Washington today because she and her husband were so generous in their philanthropy. Gwendolyn Cafritz, who died in 1988, was married to a self-made real estate developer, Maurice Cafritz. In her heydey of the 1940s and 50s, she was a social legend. Outspoken in manner and lavish in entertaining, she was a constant feature in the society pages of the local newspapers. The Cafritz's majestic art deco-style home on Foxhall Road, reputedly the

Facing page: lawns and flower beds set off the bow-fronted south side of the White House. Dinner guests to the Georgian mansion arrive at the porticoed north side.

road with the city's highest-priced real estate, has a sweeping view of Washington, black-and-white murals, mirrored walls, and a transparent dance floor lit from below. Over the years, Gwen Cafritz entertained the likes of the Duke and Duchess of Windsor, the young Jack Kennedy and his wife, countless ambassadors and senators, and even a Vice-President. She typically hosted two large parties a year and many smaller dinners for twenty-two guests. Her passing was the end of an era, a time as removed from the present-day scene as Queen Victoria's. It fell victim to the women's movement, to two-career families, and to changing times.

Today, the majority of women in Washington work. Most make serious commitments of time and energy to important causes and without them the city's cultural, civic and medical institutions would be substantially diminished. If they haven't the leisure or inclination to run a salon, however, they still like a good party! The gold service plates may be gone, but the social scene is still glittery.

The reason the stereotype hostess is extinct and the leaders of the social scene are a new breed is because Washington has changed; to understand the women in this book and others like them, you have to look at the "real" Washington. Then you can put the hostesses in the succeeding pages into the proper context. Each is a "real" Washingtonian. Each represents one of Washington's circles and each has a distinct style.

1600 Pennsylvania Avenue

The White House sets the social pace and the rest of the city marches to its beat. Sometimes the shifts are dramatic, sometimes shocking, but regularly, every four or eight years, Washingtonians take their cue from a new leader. It doesn't matter whether it's Republican or Democratic, each new administration is a gale force, blowing out old office holders, carrying in fresh faces, shaking the social establishment to its roots.

Washington's "A-List" is always official Washington, weighted to the Palace Guard, those with access to the President and First Lady. And the White House is always the number one invitation. No matter how jaded, how satiated with caviar and champagne, even the most blasé Washingtonian covets a gold-crested invitation to the White House.

The Georgian mansion is relatively small, which often surprises visitors, but there is a contagious excitement when you walk through the doors. A dinner guest might find the red-coated Marine Band playing softly on one side of the white marble entrance hall. Two eighteenth-century cut glass chandeliers illuminate the Cross Hall, which leads into all the rooms on the State Floor. The Blue Room, an oval drawing room, is the formal reception room. A ruler-straight-backed military aide presents guests. On the walls are portraits of the first seven presidents. Through the center window one sees a fountain, the South Garden, and, in the distance, the Jefferson Memorial. Who could be blasé in such a setting?

Above: a replica of the Liberty Bell; the original is housed in Independence Hall, Philadelphia.

Right: the Renaissance-style facade of the Library of Congress.

LIBRARY
of
CONGRESS
THOMAS JEFFERSON
BUILDING

Since the President is an elected official, as much as the new administration establishes its own tone, it also reflects the preference of the majority of the voters. A quick review of past presidents, is a mini-course in American history. The see-saw from temperance to frivolity is a swing in the country's mood. In the recent past the presidential wavelength has gone from barbecues and thrift to jelly beans and conspicuous razzle-dazzle. Jimmy Carter openly admired frugality and practiced it, among other ways, by carrying his own suitcase and selling the presidential yacht *Sequoia*. He took the oath of office wearing a $175 business suit purchased the week before in Americus, Georgia. He and Rosalynn served grits and ribs on the south lawn of the White House.

The Reagans' arrival was diamond-studded. Private jets roared in with Hollywood chums wearing chunks of designer diamonds and miles of mink. Jelly beans, seafood and light California cuisine were in.

These flip-flops are nothing new. It's been this way since George and Martha Washington set up temporary housekeeping in New York City while the Federal Capital was being built. They were determined to give the new office the dignity and respect it deserved; on the other hand, neither wanted the trappings of royalty or the symbols of aristocratic snobbery. Nobody knew quite what to expect at their first reception. Martha wasn't sure about protocol herself and in the end she decided to wear a simple white brocade dress for her premiere party. The President's suit was a fine fabric woven at Mount Vernon. Their guests apparently expected a far grander event, because they were more elaborately attired in ostrich feathers, rich velvets and satins, and diamond buckles. Since human nature doesn't change, it's not surprising that there were as many social climbers, gossips and critics then as there are today. After a few months of being criticized for every move, Martha Washington wrote, "I am more like a state prisoner than anything else, there is certain bounds set for me which I must not depart from … and as I cannot doe (sic) as I like I am obstinate and stay home a great deal."

She did stick to the precedents set during that initial reception, however. Each person was presented by name, then Washington moved around the room while Martha sat on a sofa and spoke quietly with the women who took turns joining her. Servants passed tea, coffee and small cakes. Promptly at nine o'clock, Mrs. Washington rose and smiled at her guests. "The General retires at nine o'clock and I usually precede him. Good night." He bowed and they left.

It was to be democracy with a small "d"!

When John and Abigail Adams moved into the half-completed White House, she resorted to hanging her wash in the great unfinished audience room. Farm animals roamed the muddy paths that served as streets, but the first lady was determined to practice the social amenities with a weekly "drawing room." The newly-established Marine Band played at the first presidential "musick" New Year's Day, 1800. Considering that the Adams moved in with the knowledge they had to vacate in the fall, their pluck is to be admired. Thomas Jefferson was waiting in the wings.

Older than the city itself, the Georgetown neighborhood (facing page) is worlds apart from the bustle and the grand monuments of the government and commercial districts.

The first night he was in the White House Adams wrote: "I pray to Heaven to bestow the best of blessings on this House and all that shall hereafter inhabit it. May none but honest and wise Men ever rule under this roof." Thirty presidents later, Franklin Delano Roosevelt had the words carved onto a White House fireplace.

Widower Thomas Jefferson thought the president's house "big enough for two emperors, one pope, and the grand lama." Washington and Adams had had essentially English tastes, whereas Jefferson imported continental ideas, furniture, plants and food – including ice cream and macaroni. With his own far-reaching interests, he drew in leading statesmen, politicians, explorers, artists and poets. One guest described an elegant dinner with not one single toast or mention of politics! The rough Capital had a population of some 3,000 with 137 clerks. It's said that the halls of Congress emptied when the horseraces were on.

The irrepressible Dolley Madison was an extravagant hostess, tireless in organizing and planning. Women in feathers, flowers and white gloves waltzed with men in lace cravats. James Madison was preoccupied with the two-year war the United States was waging with England, but Dolley worked harder than ever to divert her guests, often carrying a popular book in her hand, open at a provocative passage.

Ironically, this most social of creatures had her finest hour when she was alone. In August 1814, with the British army's arrival in Washington imminent, James Madison galloped away to support the nearby American forces. Alone in the White House, Dolley stowed the original draft of the Constitution, the Declaration of Independence, and other invaluable government papers in one small trunk. The city was being evacuated while she removed the portrait of George Washington by Gilbert Stuart. The White House burned but our history was preserved.

After fun-loving Dolley, the social pendulum swung hard. Elizabeth Monroe was pronounced "snobbish." She received only visitors to whom she had sent invitations and refused to pay calls, sending her daughter instead. James Monroe was reelected anyway. A clue as to the priorities of the times is found in a city directory: it lists one nurse, one librarian and two dancing masters.

In 1829 the popular Andrew Jackson "Old Hickory" made the record books by having the most rowdy inauguration reception. On the day of the inauguration, Washington (population about 18,000) was bursting with an estimated 10,000 visitors who had come to see Jackson take the oath of office. Hordes streamed into the White House, devoured the cakes, ice cream and orange punch, stood on chairs, broke china and tore drapes. Jackson escaped through a rear window and retreated to a nearby tavern.

If observers reached any conclusions about White House standards from that episode, they were wrong. The rough frontiersman was a widower, and suited himself by following the French precedents set by Jefferson. He entertained often and set a fancy table. The new power elite were Southern by sentiment, rich New Englanders and a growing Diplomatic corps.

Jackson's successor, Martin Van Buren, was also a widower. He lost a bid for reelection, in part, by charges that he aspired to make the White House "a palace as splendid as that of the Caesars." Opponents said he doused his whiskers with French eau de cologne, slept in a Louis XV bedstead and sipped soup with a gold spoon! Americans hadn't gotten over their dislike of royal trappings.

It was a dull social scene when James and Sarah Polk moved in in 1845. They looked upon so-called worldly pleasures as wasteful indulgences, and forbade cards, dancing and liquor. There was nothing to do at the receptions but promenade up and down the East Room and admire the new gas lights, which were still very much a novelty.

Coming to town then, Charles Dickens was unimpressed: "It is sometimes called the City of Magnificent Distances, but it might with greater propriety be termed the City of Magnificent Intentions." True enough, L'Enfant's grand plan was barely recognizable. Another visitor complained that the noise of the cows and pigs roaming free at night combined with the cacophony of dogs and cats, kept him awake. The local Southern aristocracy dominated the social scene, strolled the White House grounds at garden parties and went to the Capitol to hear their favorite speakers.

Mary Lincoln suffered over real and imagined social slights. Her only antidote was shopping. "I must dress in costly materials," she said. "The very fact of having grown up in the West subjects me to more searching observation." Some of Southern aristocracy accepted her invitations and secretly ridiculed her "attempts at Southern hospitality." A sympathetic friend wrote: "women who knew the wire-pulling at Washington, whose toilet arts and social pretensions, society-lobbying and opportunity-seeking taught them to lie in wait and rise in the social scale by intimacy at the White House, these basely laughed at the credulous woman who took counsel from them ..."

The shopping bills accumulated. History reports that when Mary Lincoln was in a good mood, she was lively, witty and charming. Despite criticism for "callous and extravagant" entertainments while the Civil War was raging, she invited the public to hear the Marine Band in the White House grounds Wednesday and Saturday afternoons and continued the customary receptions and dinners.

"During the post-Civil War decades, money became the standard of social excellence and could be offset only by official positions." The historian is describing the Grant administration. It was what Mark Twain called the "Gilded Age," for when the gilt wore off, one saw base brass. Washington was a gambler's paradise.

With hand extended as if in welcome, the portrait of George Washington (above) by Gilbert Scott greets visitors to the National Gallery. Guests at his Mount Vernon home (right) would have been assured of an equally warm reception some two hundred years ago.

Red brick sidewalks, grand Federal-style residences (facing page) and more modest Victorian houses epitomize fashionable Georgetown.

It has been suggested that Ulysses S. Grant would have been better off retiring from public life after the last Civil War battle. His two terms were racked with scandal and corruption. In an age of conspicuous consumption, Julia Grant hosted presidential parties that were just that. There was a thirty-five-course dinner for one of Queen Victoria's offspring and the doors were thrown open to the public for a reception with a "perfect river of human life" pouring in.

Comments on first ladies have always been brutal. At one reception: "Mrs. Grant stands a little way from the President – fair, fat and forty."

Julia Grant deserves one more mention. Unlike many first ladies before and after her, she was happy in the White House. Apparently in blessed ignorance of the storm clouds brewing around her husband, she wrote: "My life at the White House was like a bright and beautiful dream and we were immeasurably happy ... life ... was a garden spot of orchids."

With Rutherford B. Hayes there was another abrupt social about-face. Lucy Hayes refused to serve wine at the White House, bringing down upon herself the ridicule of society. With "Lemonade Lucy," it was said, "water flowed like wine."

Several times throughout its history Washington has been declared almost grown up. In the 1880s one resident wrote: "Within the past ten years Washington has ceased to be a village. Whether it has yet to become a city depends on the point of view. ... It has large public buildings and monuments and numerous statues; it has a mild climate, clean, well paved streets and no local politics."

Mild climate was an exaggeration. The swamp behind the White House had been filled in but the summer weather was, and is, hot and steamy. Queen Victoria's first minister to Washington, Henry Stephen Fox, was selected as "climate proof" – he had already served in Brazil.

The "cave dwellers" were overtaken in the gay nineties by very wealthy businessmen and their families who moved to town and built palaces up and down Massachusetts Avenue. A crowd of 9,000 danced at the new Pension Building for President Cleveland's first inaugural ball in 1897. The building's design set off an avalanche of criticism. Reflecting, perhaps, on his own drastic solutions, General William Sherman snorted, "The worst of it is, it is fireproof."

Cleveland, a bachelor, delighted the nation by marrying the young and lovely Frances Folsom in June, 1896. "Frank," as the President called her, was the youngest First Lady in the nation's history, but she was a poised and charming hostess. And a good guesser. As the Clevelands left the White House in 1889, she is reported to have told the servants, "I want you to take good care of all the furniture and ornaments in the house, for I want to find everything just as it is now when we come back again ... four years from today."

And they did. Thereby making Grover Cleveland the 22nd *and* 24th President of the United States.

It was Theodore Roosevelt (1901-09) who legally gave the executive mansion the name "White House." The press called the family "The Royal Roosevelts" and the eldest daughter "Princess Alice." At forty-three the youngest President at his accession (John Kennedy was younger when elected), Teddy and his wife Edith and their six energetic children burst into the White House and never stopped creating havoc.

The staff must have been wide-eyed to see roller-skating and a Chinese wrestling match in the East Room, more usually the scene of receptions, weddings and funerals. The "White House gang," Roosevelt children and friends, brought ponies and snakes into the house and decorated the presidential portraits with spitballs. There simply wasn't space for all that plus the sizable menagerie of animals, and the White House was enlarged and major renovations made.

Teddy Roosevelt practiced what he called "the strenuous life," playing tennis on the White House lawn, horseback riding, hiking and, in the winter, swimming in the icy Potomac. Edith Roosevelt was efficient, but she finally succumbed to reality and hired a secretary to handle White House social matters. Star of the show was "Princess Alice." Her marriage in 1906 to House Speaker Nicholas Longworth was one of the biggest social events in Washington in many years.

A whiff of starch and polish preceded the next first family. Helen Taft had waited for years to be First Lady, ever since she stayed there with the Hayes – family friends. Strong-

Bathed in the soft light of evening, the Jefferson Memorial casts shimmering reflections on the waters of the Tidal Basin.

willed, intelligent and ambitious, she decked out the White House doormen in livery and held twice as many lavish parties as any previous administration. It was Helen Taft who asked the mayor of Tokyo to present the American people with the 3,000 pink cherry trees which are planted around the Tidal Basin.

The Woodrow Wilsons were so serious they dispensed with the inaugural ball. Ellen Wilson, it was said, would even sit silently through dinner parties. If she was a poor hostess, she was nevertheless a boon to Washington. Her devotion was to welfare work and she personally escorted a number of congressmen through Washington's worst festering slums. Legislation to clear the slums was passed as she lay dying.

Seven months later the taciturn President met Edith Bolling Galt, a widow, and fell in love. They were married December 1915. The rather aristocratic Edith Wilson was decidedly more social than the first Mrs. Wilson and persuaded her bridegroom to reinstate the inaugural ball for his second term. During the last 17 months of his second term, Wilson was suffering from the effects of a paralytic stroke. Only his wife, doctor and closest top-level advisers saw him. The White House took on a look it has never had, before or since: the gates were closed, guards posted and window shades were drawn.

The city was now growing up rapidly. Before World War I, Washington knew the Presidents as approachable fellow citizens in a small city that still had country charm. With the war, the Capital became the mobilization center for the wealth, manpower and industry of the nation. It would take World War II before the Capital would truly become a "city," but it was getting close.

The executive mansion must have quaked with the arrival of its next occupants. Warren Gamaliel Harding (1921-23) is widely considered the worst President ever, and his administration the most corrupt. Harding accurately sized up his wife Florence, whom he nicknamed "Duchess," this way: "Mrs Harding wants to be the drum major in every band that passes."

It was "the roaring twenties" and though the Duchess followed Prohibition's ban on liquor for official parties, there was plenty of bootleg gin on the poker table upstairs. There were also toothpicks on the downstairs dining room table; Harding wouldn't reform even his table manners. The Duchess did her best, giving a constant round of parties, visiting welfare institutions and even personally guiding visitors through the public rooms of the executive mansion. As rumors of the misdeeds of Harding administration officials grew, she became frightened and asked for Secret Service protection. She also quarreled nonstop with the President, and small wonder. Known as a ladies man, his name was linked to various women, including one who wrote a book alleging that he had fathered her illegitimate daughter. It was rumored that he had young women smuggled through the back door into the White House cloakroom. As the charges of corruption circulated, Harding slipped away to all-night stag poker parties. He died of an embolism while on a speaking tour on August 2, 1923.

His successor was the complete opposite. "Silent Cal" Calvin Coolidge was in the unsociable habit of glancing at his watch mid-way through a dinner and going upstairs to bed without saying a word to his guests. "I have never been hurt by what I have not said," is one of his aphorisms. Fortunately Grace Coolidge was charming and gay; without her, White House dinners would have been unbearably grim.

Washington's "cave dwellers" looked forward to the arrival of Franklin and Eleanor Roosevelt. Here were people of their own class. Franklin was patrician by birth, well educated and endowed with an independent fortune; Eleanor was a niece of Theodore Roosevelt's. The "cave dwellers" were in for a disappointment; the Roosevelts did not care about lavish entertaining.

During the twelve Roosevelt years (1933-45), life in the White House was relaxed and informal and the executive mansion was run like a gentleman's country home. The six Roosevelt children and their families came and went, staff moved in, and there were constant overnight visitors. Mrs. Roosevelt gave a staggering number of receptions, but was notoriously indifferent to the preparations and left the running of things entirely to the staff. Guests complained privately about the terrible food and repetition of the same menus again and again. A storm of protest went up when Eleanor served the King and Queen of England hot dogs and mustard at a picnic instead of honoring them with a black-tie state dinner. In the '30s and '40s, the country wasn't yet accustomed to a First Lady who had a mind of her own and expressed it.

After the United States entered the war, White House routine changed and the Roosevelts reduced their entertaining. Wartime security regulations were set up, including machine guns on the roof and a bomb shelter in the basement.

Then, again, an about-face. Harry S. Truman would have been the first to deny himself the adjective "patrician." Rather he was typically Middle Western, a man of the people, blunt and outspoken. And Elizabeth "Bess" Truman rarely gave a public speech and had a passion for anonymity. Nine months after Truman's inauguration she went Christmas shopping at Washington department stores and wasn't even recognized. The President was a "capable" pianist and sometimes played Chopin and Mozart for his guests.

The wheel spun again. Former General Dwight David Eisenhower was elected in 1952 as a combination hero-leader and father figure. Everyone liked Ike. They liked Mamie Dowd Eisenhower, too. Americans saw a friendly woman with a spontaneous smile, who genuinely enjoyed people. She was ultra-feminine in flowered hats, colored gloves, full-skirted, fluffy dresses and anything pink. A perfectionist about entertaining, she took note of every detail.

Facing page: the serene, Gothic interior of Washington Cathedral.

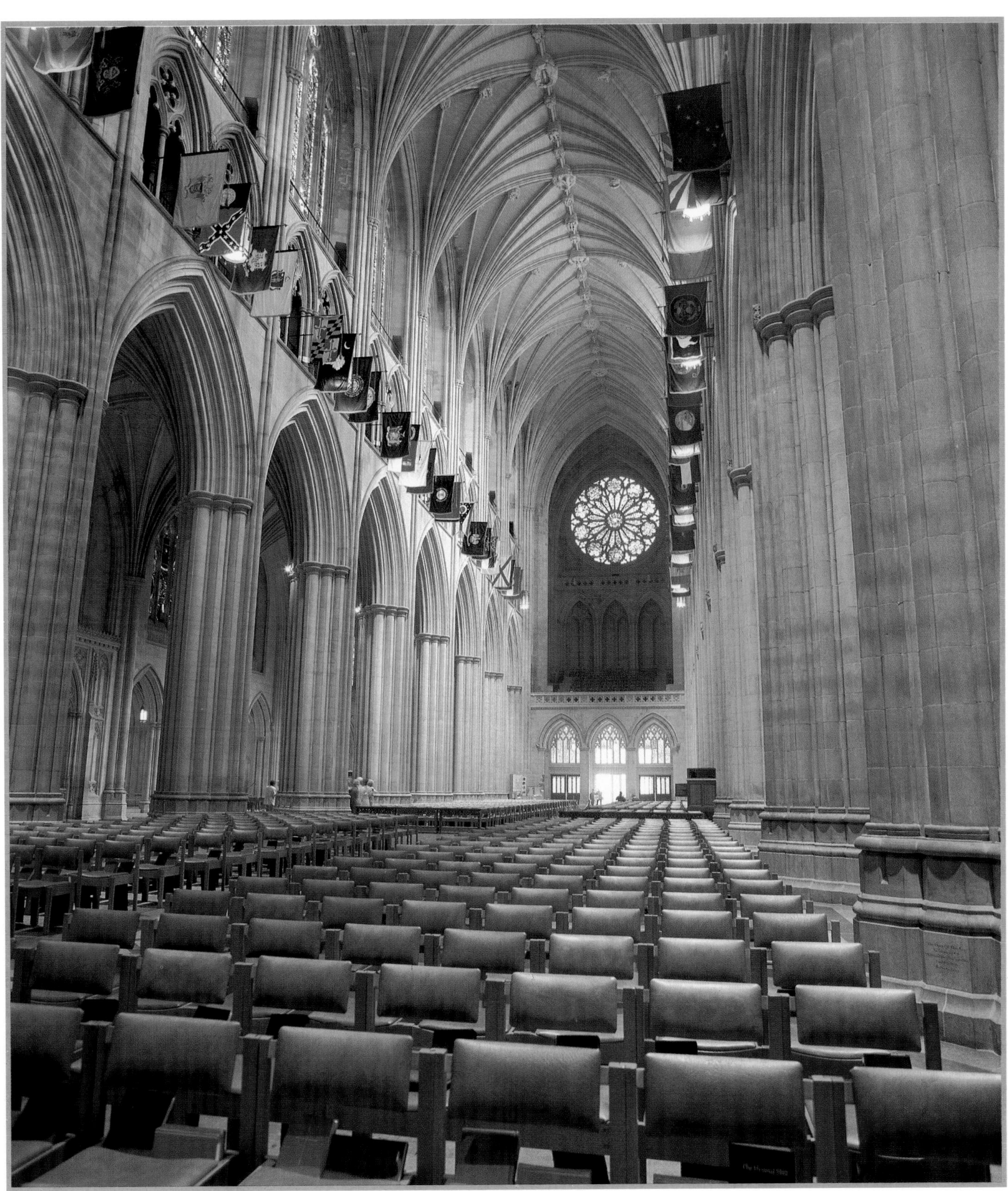

The clean, classical lines of the Jefferson Memorial (left) contrast with the embroidered dome of the Shrine of the Immaculate Conception (above).

Ike had a heart attack and major operation during his first term, so when he decided to run again, it was with the understanding that social functions would be drastically reduced. The Eisenhowers eliminated all five of the large receptions customarily included then in the winter social schedule and revamped state dinners into state luncheons.

The social tempo shifted into fast forward when John and Jacqueline Bouvier Kennedy moved into the White House in 1961. At thirty-one, she was the third youngest First Lady and initially was rather shy. Three-year-old Caroline and infant John were the youngest children of a President to live in the White House in more than sixty years. Women everywhere copied Jackie's clothes and hairdo. Her lasting legacy is the redecorated White House. When she first saw it, she told her husband, "It looks like a house where nothing has ever taken place. There is no trace of the past." She launched a program to gather furnishings of past Presidents, to make the mansion an historic showplace. And she used the White House setting to showcase the performing arts, hosting cultural galas and glittering musicales after state dinners.

"Y'all Come," was a catchphrase of the LBJ years. Lyndon Baines Johnson and Lady Bird, Texans like George and Barbara Bush, brought Texan spontaneity and friendliness to the White House. Lady Bird usually included dancing at parties because the President enjoyed it so. Teenage daughters Lynda Bird and Luci had to take Secret Service agents along on dates.

In 1897 a crowd of 3,000 danced with President Cleveland. By 1969 there had to be five inaugural balls for Richard and Pat Nixon to accommodate 300,000 celebrants. A month earlier 20-year-old Julie Nixon had married Dwight David Eisenhower II, grandson of the ex-president. The new life style at the White House was low key and quieter. The diet-conscious President lunched – usually alone – on salad and cottage cheese and often worked after dinner. Full-dress state dinners and other entertaining continued with the Nixons' daughter Patricia, in her early twenties, often acting as hostess. Most Sundays 300 people were invited to nondenominational church services in the East Room.

The country was still in shock after Nixon's resignation on August 9, 1974, but Washingtonians, resilient from experience, waited to see what Gerald and Betty Ford would be like in the White House. What was most impressive was not social style, however, but the first lady's personal courage and fortitude.

Less than two months after becoming First Lady, Betty Ford underwent a mastectomy. The openness with which she discussed her surgery comforted and inspired women around the world. She has since been equally candid about her former alcohol and chemical dependency.

Then followed the thrift, grits and ribs of the Carter years; the designer dress, seafood and light California cuisine of the Reagan years, and now the Bushes.

The Bush social style is casual chic. Heartier food like

spicy Southwestern Tex-Mex and down-home Italian, but also flowers and candles and glitzy gowns are all in. Thanks to her years as wife of the vice-president and before that ambassador to the United Nations, Mrs. Bush is undaunted by the intricate demands of White House protocol. She is a relaxed and self-confident hostess. The President is gregarious, delighting in showing friends the family's private apartment on the second floor. The Bushes are reviving a practice followed by Jimmy and Rosalynn Carter in moving the after-dinner speech and toasts to before dinner. The Reagans had moved it back. Officially the White House East Wing (the First Lady's office is in the East Wing, the President's is in the West) says only that this makes a "better flow." Unofficially the change is a blow for common sense since the toasts are likely to be more appreciated when guests are wide awake.

Children, grandchildren and dogs are in. The four Bush sons and one daughter have produced a raft of photogenic offspring who continually romp through the executive mansion. Thirty-one-pound springer spaniel Millie is the First Lady's shadow. Tennis, and jogging are popular, and when the Bushes are vacationing at Kennebunkport, Maine; boating, fishing and swimming are in.

The style is spontaneous. (Spontaneity is not easy for the Secret Service, which likes to check everything out in advance.) The Bushes often put together a last-minute dinner party with a group of old friends, afterward showing a movie in the White House screening room. Or they will get up a small party and drop in on a local ethnic restaurant.

The Bushes' entourage includes old friends from Texas and a leavening of Washingtonians they've known for years. The President and First Lady are old-timers in the Capital, with long friendships in diplomatic and political areas as well as connections with many of the socially prominent figures who run the fund-raisers or corporate-supported cultural events.

Vice-Presidents are constitutionally second fiddle, not style setters, but Dan and Marilyn Quayle apparently blend nicely into the Bushes' style. The official Vice-Presidential residence is an elaborate, secluded Victorian structure atop a hill on twelve grassy acres. There's plenty of room for tennis courts, a running track and playing fields for the three young Quayle children and two black Labradors.

More men have been elected between Sundown and Sunup than ever were elected between Sunup and Sundown.

Will Rogers

While the White House is always the center of events, there's been a change in Washington over the last two decades that affects everything from the process of passing legislation on Capitol Hill to the price of real estate to the cocktail circuit. The city itself has, at long last, become a world-class capital.

There has been an explosive growth in government – there are more than 350,000 federal employees in the Washington area, plus another 65,000 uniformed military personnel. Along with government growth there has been a twenty-year development boom and subsequent dramatic growth in the private sector – somebody has to feed and house and clothe everybody else.

The population count is swelling with foreign professionals who find the cosmopolitan air genial. There are legions of formers – former senators, congressmen and officials – who don't want to go home. "Potomac fever" is the incurable addiction to being close to the center of power. It's reached epidemic proportions despite the identity shock formers get when their phone calls aren't returned. President Lyndon Johnson used to warn aides, "Remember, you may be dancing at the ball tonight, but if things go wrong, you could be decorating a lamppost by noon tomorrow." It takes a strong grip on reality not to confuse attention with affection, as many formers have learned to their sorrow.

The economic boom is visible in the proliferation of construction against Washington's low skyline. There are countless new luxury office buildings in the downtown area, ten new museums, numerous four-star, expense-account restaurants, and top-of-the-line hotels. The Kennedy Center, opened in 1971, has made the city a "must" for performing artists. Sally Chapoton says the city is much more sophisticated today than it was when her husband first came to Washington in 1969 and she attributes that largely to the Kennedy Center.

Georgetown has also changed over the past decades; although the exterior look remains the same because of a strict preservation code, on weekend nights it is crowded and raucous with the invading young and restless college-age kids who are out to party. During the week Georgetown reverts, once again, to the quiet place moviegoers expect, an oasis of well-scrubbed stately portals, high-ceilinged drawing rooms, and well-groomed young matrons in tennis whites. This is still the preferred roost for "cave dwellers," but it is not the dinner party power center it was in the Kennedy era. And it is not where the boom is showing.

That's happening in a chain of desirable neighborhoods where mega-houses are springing up. Some are built on sites of million-dollar "knockdown" houses, homes purchased for the location and then demolished. Typically, the new houses are multimillion-dollar brick colonials: three-car garages for Mercedes, Jaguars and BMWs, a tennis court, swimming pool and pool house out back, creamy Italian marble in the multi-storied entrance hall, enormous master bedrooms, a fireplace by the whirlpool tub in the master bath, and "Gone With the Wind" staircases – all wired with security systems and intercoms.

Boom town Washington is a hard-working place. The sleepy Southern ways disappeared, once and for all, with the opening salvos of World War II. Politicians are, by definition,

Facing page: an eight on the Potomac.

Facing page: elegance and sophistication are the hallmarks of parties given by Washington's hostesses. Above: 20th-century exhibits in the National Museum of American Art.

super-achievers. So are the aggressive, ambitious men and women in all those rippling circles.

Because so much of government depends on personal contacts, the distinction between business and pleasure is often fuzzy. From September through June, social life in Washington is a triathlon of state dinners, receptions and black-tie fund-raisers. If you are in the political-media-social fast lane, you can stay on the merry-go-round until you drop.

Workaholics often begin the day with two working breakfasts, go on to power lunches or brown-bag lunches while returning the morning's phone calls, and book themselves up to as many as fifteen parties a week. Which explains why the "nightcap," the after-dinner brandy, has virtually disappeared. This is an early-to-bed town.

Contrary to what cynics say, Washington is also a place where many of its residents believe that what they do makes a difference to the country and its people. Feeling that you count is wonderfully energizing. As much as ambition for power motivates some people, and ambition for prominence or fortune drives others, this feeling of participation, of making a difference, is what really propels most Washingtonians. A lot is sacrificed, but a lot is gained in the exhilaration of achievement.

F. Scott Fitzgerald said, "The rich are different from us." "Yes," Ernest Hemingway retorted, "they have more money." Well, Washington politicians and all those attendant circles *are* different. They work in the most important capital in the world. Or, at least, that's how they see it.

"Inside the beltway," meaning the sixty-four-mile loop around the city, is the metaphor for the Washington point of view. "Outside the beltway" is the boondocks, that is, the rest of the country. Well, inside the beltway the most important commodity is access. The struggle for power and the interplay of personalities are fundamental in a democracy. That's as true today as it was in 1800. But the pressure is on as it never has been before.

It's a well-behaved feeding frenzy, with one group subsisting on the other. Constituents and lobbyists hurl a nonstop

barrage against congressmen to get votes and against officials to get leverage. Congressmen need lobbyists for donations to campaigns and for honoraria, fees for making appearances and delivering speeches. Journalists need congressmen for stories. Some journalists also take fees from lobbyists for speeches. And congressmen need journalists for good press to impress the folks back home!

Giant corporations and associations want access to the Federal government no matter who is in office and therefore they need Washington offices. The defense industry, banking, savings and loans, insurance, oil, all need access. Associations now rank as the third largest industry here, just behind government and tourism, and every association and corporation has lobbyists – whole armies of people, all vying for the chance to chat with someone influential about a project or a product or a proposal.

Since a lot of that interaction takes place after the end of the business day, it follows that corporate lobbyists are now the really big party givers in Washington. Corporations regard parties as marketing tools, along with television and print advertising. And since the big corporations have the budget and the incentive in a situation where the stakes may be a multibillion-dollar contract, the parties can be spectacular. Because the events have taken on such importance, their planning is too crucial to leave in the hands of amateurs. A new career is that of the professional party planner whose job is to win friends and curry favor in high places on a magnified scale.

Until recently the only professionals sending out invitations to the ritual banquets of official Washington were the White House and embassy social secretaries. A good social secretary could guide a new ambassador past the social pitfalls. Now organizing parties and events is big business.

One of this book's hostesses is Gretchen Poston, who is partner in an events planning/public relations business WashingtonInc., with clients like Coca-Cola, ABC, and a number of trade associations. This multimillion-dollar firm's growth epitomizes the transition many Washington women have made. Twenty years ago three bored housewives – Ellen Proxmire, wife of Wisconsin Senator William Proxmire; Barbara Boggs, wife of lobbyist Tom Boggs and daughter-in-law of Congresswoman Lindy Boggs; and Gretchen, wife of attorney Raymond Poston, founded a wedding planning business as a lark. Working from home with a rented typewriter, they earned $35 for the first wedding. After two years of dealing with emotional parents, they branched out and began arranging conventions. By the mid-'70s, the women had become respected members of the business community. They, and a fourth partner, Harriet Schwartz, arrange a seated dinner for 2,200 with less nervousness than some folks feel facing a buffet for twenty. In addition to forty full-time staff, the firm keeps on-call battalions of young men

A cloudless sky throws the elegant lines of the capitol into sharp relief.

NW O ST

and women who communicate by walkie-talkie, numerous translators, transportation coordinators capable of getting crowds on and off buses, set builders and even a brass band.

Without those extensive props, the private party giver can take consolation from the fact that the same catastrophies befall giant parties as tiny ones, and she can also take a cue as to quick recoveries. One particularly cold winter night Gretchen managed a seated dinner for 120 in a tent attached to the Canadian Embassy. When heaters failed, shivering guests simply put on their coats, donned socks passed out by the ambassador's wife, and probably drank a little more than normal so the goodwill thermometer rose as the temperature plummeted.

Big institutional sponsors spare no expense and nothing is left to chance. When 6,000 international bankers check into town, their events are as carefully staged and rehearsed as a Broadway production. Even with 150 limousine companies in town, stretch limos have to be imported from New York to keep up with the on-the-go financiers. There's even a daily newspaper just for them, listing the parties so people can pick and choose. With twenty or thirty events a day, there is a constant semaphore-like exchange of business cards over the ice sculptures.

Charity benefits dominate the social scene in Washington and it is, by and large, corporations that are buying the tickets and underwriting the events. Corporate money underwrites Kennedy Center fund-raisers, the Symphony Ball, the Cancer Ball, the Opera Ball, even museum openings. National Art Gallery Director J. Carter Brown is a genius at wooing corporations, first to fund major art shows and then to underwrite the opening night parties preceding the shows.

Charity fund-raisers are run by a cadre of socially active women like Pamela Howar, Cathy Martens, Sally Chapoton and Carol Foley. They are volunteers, but as serious as professionals about raising a quarter of a million dollars in one night. The Symphony Ball, Washington's only white tie ball, raised half a million dollars in 1988. To reach those kinds of goals, these women smilingly and fiercely compete for charity dollars; corporate underwriters have to be persuaded to make donations and friends have to be cajoled into bartering tickets – I'll do your event if you'll do mine. It helps to have connections in the race to snare patrons and honorary sponsors. The President and Mrs. Bush are top of the list, naturally, followed by important ambassadors.

Many women are both full-time professionals and serious volunteers. Carol Lascaris is an award-winning interior designer with offices all over the world, and she has chaired the National Symphony Ball. Penne Korth is a Washington associate with Sotheby's, the international art and auction house. She was co-chair of the Bush Presidential Inaugural. Alta Leath has a jewelry business, the Altomar Collection, with a shop at the Watergate Hotel and another in Dallas. Jayne Ikard is a full-time consultant. Aniko Gaal is vice-president for Fashion and Public Relations for Garfinkel's, Washington's premiere specialty store. They are all active in the community.

To give a charity event a boost, the charity committees hook in with Washington's glitterati – the embassies. There's social cachet in using an embassy residence for small pre-gala dinners, teas, luncheons and fashion shows. One of the most desirable residences is the elegant Villa Firenze – residence of Italian Ambassador Rinaldo Petrignani and his wife Anne Merete. The lawn is easily tented in all but the dead of winter and the Fortuny-draped reception rooms are large. Between all the different functions held there each year, eight to ten thousand people are entertained at Villa Firenze. Mrs. Petrignani doesn't keep a count.

An influential group of Washington hostesses are "wives of." Washington's official world is still a male preserve; there are only twenty-three women in the 535-member House of Representatives, two out of a hundred Senators, one out of nine Supreme Court Justices. "Congressional wives are a very close-knit group," says Alta Leath, whose husband Marvin was first elected to Congress in 1978. "We empathize with one another. It's a special kind of club because your life changes when he's elected. There are certain demands on your time and your family's time. Perhaps it's like being married to a doctor, but a doctor doesn't live in a fishbowl."

The circles of congressional and diplomatic wives bump into one another and residential Washington through a number of clubs and organizations set up for the express purpose of introducing them to one another.

The bible in seating guests, addressing envelopes with correct titles, order of precedence (who sits next to the hostesses, and on down the table) is "The Green Book," an annual social list of the White House staff, executive federal offices, diplomatic corps, senators and congressmen and then the social list, complete with zip codes. Finally there are social guidelines, such as "At a dinner the Hostess makes the move to leave the table, and the Guest of Honor the move to leave the house first." (If the Hostess left the house first, it might raise eyebrows.) Listing is by invitation and not everyone who could be in wishes to be, but most do.

Some of the names in the Green Book will be gone with the next election, but many have staying power. Washington is full of contradictions. This is a transient town, people come and go, and at the same time there are many here whose roots go back several generations. Mariana Grove is a fourth-generation native Washingtonian on her father's side, granddaughter of a Panamanian diplomat on her mother's side. These third- and fourth-generation names are not necessarily seen in newspaper headlines though they may move in and out of government service. They are certainly not immune to the lure of political power, but they take a longer view: senators come and go, so do presidents. Meanwhile the old-timers definitely find a sense of community

Facing page: each spring, the delicate pink of cherry blossom is to be seen all over the city.

and continuity here. And they, also, are "real" Washingtonians.

Only a handful of the 144 embassies in Washington are on Massachusetts Avenue, but it is called "Embassy Row" and there are enough diplomatic residences there for frequent queues of flag-bedecked limousines to create traffic jams. Locals vociferously resent "diplomatic immunity," meaning diplomats are exempt from local parking laws, as well as local taxes.

For years embassies provided the bedrock of Washington glamor by entertaining lavishly. There used to be three large embassy parties a night, each with dinner and dancing. Once a year the British invited 1,500 people for clotted cream and strawberries at a garden party celebrating the Queen's birthday. And in the '70s Iranian Ambassador Ardeshir Zahedi sometimes threw three or four parties a week for 700 to 800 guests each.

Now, as one wag put it, there's less roe on embassy row. Weakened currencies, faltering economies and even revolutions have reshaped the global power structure, and terrorism has required the addition of metal detectors at embassy doors – a nightmare with metallic, sequined evening gowns. Another reason embassies are toning it down has to do with a change in what's considered news. The *Washington Post* and the defunct *Washington Star* used to cover parties with almost reverential awe at what was worn and eaten. The printed guest list and gushing description could be sent home to prove the ambassador had his nose to the grindstone. Without press clippings, it's more difficult to make a case for extravagance.

Finally, there's less sparkle because some of the new generation of diplomats don't see entertainment on a massive scale as effective. These people look at their jobs as political positions, and try to establish access by making connections within the administration and media powers.

There are still brilliant parties. The "Big Three" that have always been powerful and influential are the British, French and Italian, depending on the ambassador. Other embassies become important if the ambassador and his wife are especially well-liked. And the Dean of the diplomatic corps, the ambassador who has served in Washington longest, represents the corps at White House and other functions, bringing visibility to his country, whether large or small. Budget-conscious embassies throw smallish dinner parties, supplying the food themselves and hiring a caterer to bring in waiters and dessert.

Hang a lamb chop in the window and they'll come running.

Perle Mesta

That immutable rule was the wisdom of Perle Mesta, a sparkling fixture on the Washington social scene in the 1950s and '60s, appointed Ambassador to Luxemburg by Harry Truman and source of a Broadway musical based on her life, "Call Me Madam."

Above: the National Gallery of Art. Right: Daniel Burnham's Grand Union Station, which now houses the National Visitor Center.

To a lamb chop you might add a decent bar, a few high-profile names and a clean house. It helps to light candles, put flowers around and play soft music. The secret to success is mixing and matching variations on those elements, whether the party is being given by the First Lady, a professional party planner, or a Washington hostess.

The one essential the party giver must have, money can't buy: charm. Every single hostess ever described as successful has had charm. Charm means welcoming guests with genuine enthusiasm. It means listening carefully to each guest, not scanning the crowd over the person's shoulder. It means looking after each guest as if he or she were the most important person in the room, making that person totally comfortable and relaxed.

Above: a studious silence suffuses a reading room in the Jefferson building of the Library of Congress.
Facing page: Georgetown town houses.

Dolley Madison was a charming hostess because she pleased her guests by never forgetting a face or name, and made a point of serving refreshments even to her husband's most bitter enemies. Bess Truman was looking after her guests, and being charming, when she sent a note down the head table to the President reminding him that the shy dinner partner he was ignoring was a noted atomic scientist.

A charming hostess keeps her cool and doesn't make her guests uncomfortable because there's a domestic crisis brewing. Gail Berendzen does every kind of entertaining with husband Richard, President of American University, so naturally something occasionally does go wrong. But she is unflappable. Once she was preparing a light ladies luncheon – salad and soup – when a glass fell into the garbage disposal and proceeded to spew needle-sharp fragments all over the food. "I ran to the nearest fast food place," she smiles, "and bought buckets of chicken." Another time the stove blew out just before a Shakespeare Debate dinner, to which four Supreme Court justices and officials from the British Embassy and Folger Shakespeare Library had been invited. "The caterer drove off in a rush and came back with another stove and finished cooking the dinner. But the beef was close to raw. So I went around telling people this was the way the Elizabethans ate it. Sally Chapoton didn't make her guests nervous simply because she forgot to turn the oven on and the roast was raw at dinner time. She sliced it up and sautéed it. After all, confessions do not necessarily put guests at ease.

Jayne Ikard recalled years later why she particularly liked one hostess: "Going up the steps to her house you were on a personal high. You felt you looked great; you were smart, intelligent and clever. Some hostesses have one person as the star; everybody else is a prop. I go to some parties, and

I feel it's about the hostess and the guest of honor and why are you crowding their act?"

A few high profile names as guests are glitter dust at a Washington party. The aphorism is that power is an aphrodisiac. Proximity to news, in the Capital, is a strong stimulant. A ploy as old as the real "cave dwellers" is to lure Very Important Person A by telling him VIP B will be at the party. When A accepts, call B quickly and lure him with A. A good news week helps a party. No one prays for an international crisis, but if one just happens to coincide with a dinner party where the guest list includes a member of the Senate Foreign Relations Committee, that's lucky timing for the hostess. A guest associated in any way with the White House is high profile. And he or she doesn't have to be that elevated. An assistant network news producer moves to the A-List when the network news anchor is rumored to be unhappy.

A good party is held in a "safe" house, meaning that not one word of the conversation will be repeated outside the walls. At a good party both dinner partners are interesting.

If a Hollywood director wanted to stage a "real" party in a private Washington home, the scenario might read as follows. The invitation is specific, this is a "Cocktail buffet," meaning there will be hot food, more than nibbles. Since the hours of the party come after six o'clock, the invitation has specified what should be worn. "Informal" in the lower right hand corner of a card means afternoon dress for ladies and dark suits for the men. In the lower left hand corner "Regrets only" followed by a telephone number is acceptable, although not as dignified as R.S.V.P.

Because this is large party, there is valet parking at the front door. A butler in the foyer is directing guests to the host, in a dark suit, and hostess, wearing a silk designer short dress, and good, but not overwhelming, jewelry. The house has been built with entertaining in mind and the spacious rooms are designed to ensure an easy flow of guests. Furnishings are eclectic, but antique English is the dominant style. "Most of our architecture in Washington is based on English prototypes and so antique English furniture looks best in most homes," suggests Mariana Grove, co-founder of a Washington firm specializing in antique English furniture. The air is fragrant from masses of flowers, and from potpourri and perfume. Fragile Greek myrtle and glycerine-treated boxwood topiaries bring more color in the room. A string quartet out on the flagstone terrace is a soft backdrop. Down broad steps, a yellow-and-white striped tent covers the manicured lawn – just in case of showers.

Guests include a senator from a fairly important state, a diplomat from a fairly important country, a journalist who is a talking head – a regular commentator on a TV talk show, one or two New Yorkers, assorted art buffs, old friends and perhaps a Hollywood snazzy for glamor.

As everyone relaxes over cocktails, news, views and favors circulate faster and faster and the noise level rises. Party regulars don't need to ask for a specific drink. The White House supplements its staff with a coterie of freelance butlers, fixtures themselves on the party circuit, who are as discreet as intelligence operatives. They know without asking who wants white wine or vodka and tonics from the silver trays.

Because most private entertaining is done at home, for many of Washington's busy women caterers can be lifesavers. Not everyone uses them, of course, but many do. The food can be first-rate and the service unobtrusive. Caterers will actually bring in and serve a large dinner party without even entering the house's kitchen. They set up stoves and necessary equipment in the garage or someplace else out of sight. For the popular cocktail buffet, the party these days is organized around "stations" – small tables stationed in several parts of the house or around the terrace and pool.

In the '70s a Washington party-goer was bound to find a steamship round of beef and ham being carved at opposite sides of a huge buffet table and in between silver chafing dishes filled with egg rolls, Swedish meatballs, sweet and sour meatballs, miniature franks in puff pastry and chicken livers wrapped inside bacon. By the late '70s raw vegetables and raw bars were on the ascendancy, and in the early '80s it was small potatoes stuffed with caviar or phyllo dough stuffed with feta cheese and spinach.

Today, accommodation is made for those who are calorie and cholesterol conscious. At our Hollywood-staged party the stations will offer food from all over the world and some hearty, homey classics. With a nod to the White House, there are jalapeno cornbread biscuits, leaves of radicchio instead of tortillas to wrap around fillings for cold enchiladas, and chicken or beef fajitas. Rounds of apple or spears of endive replace bread for canapes. New favorites are tartare of raw tuna or salmon, spicy cold Asian pasta salad, Indian curry, Caribbean grilled shrimp, or tenderloin of beef smoked so that it can be eaten without a sauce.

That's one party scenario. Variations are as endless as the imagination. You are cordially invited to attend fifteen different parties, ranging from the formal black-tie dinner to a poolside supper, each given by a real Washington Hostess.

Facing page: Washington Cathedral.

Scullers on the Potomac silhouetted in the evening light.

· Mrs Climis Lascaris ·

Carol Lascaris is an award-winning interior designer whose credits are extraordinary. She has designed private homes, commercial offices, museums, yachts, embassies and palaces! Carol and her husband Climis founded Lascaris Design Group, Inc. in 1979; today the firm maintains offices all over the world. Projects include the Royal Pavilion at the Alia International Airport in Amman, Jordan, and the National Museum of Women in the Arts in Washington, for which Carol won the 1987 Historic Preservation and Architecture Award given by the American Institute of Architects. When she is in town and entertaining friends, Carol likes to serve Greek dishes. Her husband is Greek, of course, but also she says she has never met anyone who doesn't love Greek food. The Lascarises are a team in the kitchen. "He remembers little things from watching his grandmother and mother," she says, "and these are his grandmother's recipes." Besides being delicious, Greek food is healthy and nourishing, using lots of vegetables and having no cholesterol because only olive oil is used. Carol is active in church and community affairs. She is chairing the 1990 National Museum of Women in the Arts 7th Annual Benefit Gala and is active in fund-raising for Wolf Trap Farm Park in Virginia – the nation's only national park for the performing arts.

AVOGOLEMONO SOUPA

INGREDIENTS

1 whole chicken
1 cup Uncle Ben's rice
1 can College Inn chicken stock
3 eggs
½ cup freshly squeezed lemon juice

METHOD

In a large pan, boil the chicken in enough water to cover for 1 hour and then remove. Bone the chicken and cut the meat into cubes. Set aside.

Add the uncooked rice to the chicken stock and simmer until cooked. Separate the eggs. Using an electric mixer, whip the whites until stiff. Hand whisk the yolks separately and then combine the two. Add the lemon juice to the egg mixture a few drops at a time and mix thoroughly using an electric mixer. Add 6 ladles full of the warm chicken stock slowly to the egg mixture. Add the chicken meat and serve immediately.

RED SNAPPER (COLD PSARI)

Serves: 8

INGREDIENTS

Coriander
2 celery stalks
1 medium onion
2 carrots
1 bay leaf
2 cups white wine
5 cups water
Juice of 1 lemon

When entertaining, Carol Lascaris likes to serve Greek food, which she finds delicious as well as nourishing and healthy. This elegantly laid table features a tempting spread of Red Snapper, Keftedas, Youvarelakia, Greek Salad and Avogolemono Soupa.

1 tsp salt
1 tbsp black peppercorns
1 red snapper, approximately 4lbs

Mayonnaise Sauce

1/4 cup olive oil
1 tsp Dijon mustard
1 egg yolk
2 tsps lemon juice
Salt and pepper
3/4 cup mazola vegetable oil

METHOD

Combine the first ten ingredients in a poacher, cover and boil for 30 minutes. Place the red snapper in the poacher, cover again and slow boil for another 30 minutes. Let the fish cool in the stock for several hours. When completely cold, lift the fish out and, using a small, sharp knife, skin it carefully, leaving the head and tail on.

Mix all the mayonnaise ingredients in a blender, adding the oil gradually. Place the red snapper on a serving plate and decorate with cucumbers, parsley, watercress and lemon. Serve with the mayonnaise.

KEFTEDAS

Serves: 8

INGREDIENTS

2 slices white bread, soaked in milk to cover
2lbs ground beef
1 large onion
1 cup Parmesan cheese
Salt
Pepper
Oregano
1 cup ouzo
1 cup chopped parsley
Flour
Mazola oil

METHOD

Squeeze the milk out of the bread. Using your hands, mash all the ingredients except the flour and oil together in a large bowl and form into small meatballs. Roll the balls in flour and fry in mazola oil until browned and cooked through.

YOUVARELAKIA

Serves: 8

INGREDIENTS

2lbs ground meat
1 cup rice
2 yellow onions, finely chopped
1/2 cup flour
3 tbsps chopped mint and parsley
1/2 tbsp dried dill
1 tsp salt
2 cups water
2 tbsps butter
2 eggs
Juice of 1 lemon

METHOD

Mix the meat, rice, onion, flour, mint, parsley, dill and salt together thoroughly and form into small, football-shaped meatballs. Bring the water to a boil in a large frying pan with a little salt. Add the butter and the meatballs and simmer for 45 minutes.

To prepare the sauce, separate the eggs. Beat the whites until firm with an electric mixer. Beat the egg yolks until foamy and then blend the two together slowly with the lemon juice. Pour this sauce over the cooked, drained meatballs and serve.

GREEK SALAD

Serves: 8

INGREDIENTS

4 large tomatoes
2 large cucumbers
2 medium onions
1 cup feta cheese, crumbled
1/2 cup black Greek olives
Olive oil
Red wine vinegar
Salt and pepper to taste

Facing page: Greek Salad.

METHOD

Quarter the tomatoes and then halve each quarter. Peel and dice the cucumbers. Peel the onion and slice into thin rings. Mix all the ingredients together thoroughly and serve.

GALAKTOBOUREKO (CREAM PIE)

Serves: 8

INGREDIENTS

5½ cups milk
Peel of ½ lemon
9 eggs
1¼ cups sugar
3oz rice flour
2oz fine semolina
1 cup heavy cream
1 tsp vanilla extract
1lb frozen phyllo dough
12oz unsalted butter, melted

Syrup

2¼ cups sugar
9oz water
1 cinnamon stick
2 cloves
Juice and peel of ½ lemon

METHOD

In a large saucepan, boil the milk with the lemon peel, then remove the peel. Beat the eggs with the sugar until they are a pale lemony color. Add the rice flour and the semolina and mix well. Over a low heat, pour the egg mixture gradually into the hot milk, stirring constantly. Heat this combination for 3-4 minutes, or until it reaches the consistency of heavy cream. Remove the pan from the heat and stir in the cream and vanilla extract.

Preheat the oven to 350°. Grease a 12x14x2-inch baking pan. Place in a sheet of phyllo dough, with the edges hanging over the side. Brush the sheet with melted butter. Repeat this procedure until ⅔ of the phyllo dough has been used. Pour the cream filling into the phyllo case. Fold the edges of the sheets over the filling. Cover with the remaining sheets, brushing each one with butter. With

Right: an attractive floral display enhances a well-laid table, while grapes and fresh strawberries add color and serve as a foil to the richness of a dessert such as Galaktoboureko.

a sharp knife, make lengthwise cuts through the top layer. Bake the pie in the preheated oven for 90 minutes.

Meanwhile, make the syrup by combining all the ingredients in a saucepan and boiling them together for 10 minutes. Let the syrup cool and remove the lemon peel and cinnamon stick. Remove the pie from the oven and immediately pour the syrup over it. Let the pie cool and cut into square- or diamond-shaped pieces.

GREEK CHOCOLATE MOUSSE

Serves: 8

INGREDIENTS

2 sticks sweet butter
¾ cup confectioners' sugar
6 eggs
10oz Baker's all natural semisweet or German semisweet chocolate
1 cup chopped walnuts
¼ cup Cognac
1 tbsp vanilla extract

METHOD

Beat the butter with the confectioners' sugar for about 5 minutes, until it is white colored. Separate the eggs. Add the yolks to the butter mixture one by one, beating continuously for about 5 minutes. In a double boiler, melt the chocolate over hot water. Let it cool slightly, then pour gradually into the butter mixture, beating well until mixed. Add the chopped walnuts, Cognac and vanilla extract. In a small bowl beat the egg whites with a mixer at high speed, until stiff peaks form. Carefully fold the whites into the mousse mixture. Grease a ring mold with corn oil, pour the mixture into the mold and refrigerate until ready to serve. This mousse is better if made the day before serving.

Galaktoboureko and Greek Chocolate Mousse – two dessert dishes that taste as good as they look.

The statue of The Father of His Country in the George Washington Masonic National Memorial.

· Mrs. Brandon Grove ·

Mariana Grove epitomizes two of the Capital's circles – she is a fourth-generation Washingtonian on her father's side, the bilingual granddaughter of a Panamanian diplomat on her mother's side. Her guest list ranges from Washington school chums to family friends, diplomats, and business contacts. Co-founder of the Washington firm Flemming and Meers, specialists in antique English furniture, Mariana is married to Brandon Hambright Grove, Jr., former ambassador to Zaire and now Director of the Foreign Service Institute. Mariana's daughter Michele Parsons lives in New York. One of her four stepchildren is Catherine Cheremeteff Grove, a graduate of La Varenne, the well-known school of cooking in Paris. Catherine is executive assistant to Jean Louis Palladin, whose restaurant at the Watergate is world-famous. The dishes prepared by Catherine find an incomparable setting in the light-filled drawing room of the Groves' apartment. The room is focused around a Chinese Coromandel screen.

A member of the Women's Committee of the Corcoran Gallery of Art, Mariana also serves on the Women's Committee of the Washington Opera and was Chairman of the 1987 Hispanic Designers Fashion Show.

TUNA TARTAR SERVED ON CRISPY POTATO ROUNDS

Serves: 12

INGREDIENTS

2 large Russet potatoes, peeled
2 tbsps lemon juice
12oz tuna fillet, as fresh as possible
3 tbsps soy sauce
1 tbsp lime juice
1 tbsp curry powder, more if desired
2 tbsps finely chopped fresh dill
2 tbsps finely sliced chives
1/4 cup extra-virgin olive oil
Fine sea salt and freshly ground pepper to taste
Olive oil for frying
Fresh dill sprigs, to garnish

METHOD

Using a mandoline, julienne the potatoes very thinly and place in a bowl with the lemon juice. Cover and set aside until ready to fry. You may not use all the potato, but it is better to have extra.

Using a sharp, thin-bladed knife, cut the tuna fillet into 1/4 -inch dice. Place in a bowl with the soy sauce, lime juice, curry powder, chopped dill, chives, 1/4 cup extra-virgin olive oil and salt and pepper to taste. Mix gently, cover and refrigerate for at least 2, and up to 4 hours.

Meanwhile, shape and fry the potato rounds. First drain the potato julienne and squeeze out any excess liquid. In

Ceviche of Scallops with Lime, Cilantro and Olive Oil (left) and Tuna Tartar Served on Crispy Potato Rounds (upper right).

a medium-sized non-stick skillet, heat 2 tbsps olive oil for about 3 minutes over a high heat. Once the pan is hot, remove it from the heat and arrange a thin layer of the julienne potatoes to cover the bottom of the pan completely. Try to avoid leaving any holes in the potato cake, adding more potatoes if necessary. Season with salt and pepper, return the pan to the heat and fry the potato cake for about 3 minutes, until golden brown. If the potatoes are browning too quickly, turn the heat down slightly. Using two spatulas, flip the potato cake over carefully and cook for a further 3 minutes, until the other side is also golden brown. Drain the cooked potato cake on paper towels. Once it is cool enough to touch, cut the potato cake into as many rounds as possible using a 1½-inch cookie cutter. Continue to cook the remaining potato julienne in this fashion, until you have formed at least 12 rounds.

To serve, place a small portion of the tuna tartar on top of each potato round and garnish with a sprig of fresh dill. Serve immediately to prevent the rounds becoming soggy.

QUAIL EGGS IN BRIOCHE WITH OSCIETRE CAVIAR

Makes: 12 portions

INGREDIENTS

12-15 quail eggs (12 needed but extra useful in case any break when handled)
About 12 ¼-inch slices of brioche or other sweet white bread
Vegetable oil for greasing cookie sheet or baking pan
Freshly ground black pepper
3oz (about 12 teaspoons) Oscietre caviar

METHOD

Preheat the oven to 400°. Preheat broiler if separate from oven. If you are inexperienced at opening quail eggs, first remove the top of the shells so the contents can be added quickly to the brioche shapes when needed. To do this, hold the egg flatter end up, and carefully peel away the top quarter of each shell with your fingertips. Begin by gently slicing through the shell or lightly tapping it crosswise a quarter of the way down from the top with a sharp paring knife. Place the opened eggs carefully in a small bowl and set aside.

Use a 3-inch cookie cutter to cut out 12 geometric shapes from the brioche slices. Cut out a hole in the center of each using a 1-inch cookie cutter. Grease a cookie sheet or baking pan and heat it in the preheated oven for about 1 minute, until hot. Remove from the oven and arrange the brioche shapes on it in a single layer. Using a teaspoon place one quail egg in the center of each brioche shape. Return the sheet or pan to the oven and bake for 2 minutes, then broil for a few seconds about 4 inches from the heat source, until the brioche is lightly toasted and the egg whites are opaque (the yolks should still be very runny). Remove from the broiler, and season with pepper.

Transfer the brioche shapes to a heated platter. Using two teaspoons, mold the caviar by the teaspoonful into 12 oval-shaped quenelles. Place one on top of each brioche shape, beside the egg. Serve immediately.

POPPY SEED WONTON BASKETS WITH FRESH JUMBO LUMP CRABMEAT

Serves: 12

INGREDIENTS

Baskets

15 or more wonton wrappers
1 egg yolk, lightly beaten
Vegetable oil for deep-frying
1 tbsp sweet and sour sauce
2 tbsps poppy seeds

Filling

1 cup (about ¼lb) jumbo lump crabmeat, picked over
2 tbsps very finely sliced chives
2 tbsps minced fresh chervil
2 tbsps extra-virgin olive oil
1 tsp lemon juice
Fine sea salt and freshly ground pepper to taste
12 whole chervil sprigs, to garnish

Facing page: Quail Eggs in Brioche with Oscietre Caviar, Poppy Seed Wonton Baskets with Fresh Jumbo Lump Crabmeat, and Buckwheat Blinis with Caviar Sour Cream Sauce and Salmon Roe.

METHOD

Use a 2-inch cookie cutter to cut the wonton wrappers into circles, keeping the wrappers covered when not in use to prevent them drying out. Invert a small shot glass or other small cup-shaped object, whose flat surface is about ½inch in diameter. Place a wonton circle on top of the inverted glass and press it down to form a basket shape. Seal the folds with some of the egg yolk, pressing lightly until the shape holds. Remove and set aside, uncovered. Repeat with all the wonton circles.

Meanwhile, heat the vegetable oil in a heavy saucepan to about 375°. Gently submerge each basket into the oil, working in batches, and fry for about 2 minutes, until golden brown on all sides. Remove from the oil and drain on paper towels. Once cooled, dip the top edge of each basket lightly into the sweet and sour sauce. Next dip the same edge into the poppy seeds, pressing so the seeds adhere. Set aside.

Combine all the filling ingredients in a medium-sized bowl and mix gently with a spoon. Season to taste. Fill each wonton basket with some of the crabmeat filling and garnish with a sprig of chervil. Serve immediately.

FRESH BELON OYSTERS ON THE HALF SHELL

Serves: 12

INGREDIENTS

Fresh seaweed, to garnish serving platter (optional)
3 quarts water mixed with 4 tbsps coarse sea salt, to blanch the seaweed (optional)
Ice bath for the blanched seaweed (optional)
12 large Belon oysters
¼ cup sherry vinegar
½ tsp finely chopped shallots
1 lemon, segmented

METHOD

If using the seaweed garnish, blanch it for 1 minute, until bright green in color, in the rapidly boiling salted water. Drain the seaweed immediately and plunge into the prepared ice bath. Allow to cool, then drain, cover with damp paper towels and refrigerate. This can be done up to one hour in advance.

Served on a bed of seaweed, Fresh Belon Oysters on the Half Shell (left) is a sophisticated yet simple dish. Their delicate flavor is enlivened by an equally simple mignonette sauce.

To shuck the oysters, first scrub the outer shell of each oyster thoroughly under cold running water, then open each one using an oyster knife. With a paring knife, dislodge the oyster from the muscle and leave it in the bottom half of the shell. Discard the top shell.

Make a mignonette sauce by combining the vinegar and the finely chopped shallots in a small serving bowl. Arrange a bed of the seaweed on a serving platter and place the oysters on top. Arrange the lemon segments around the edges and the mignonette sauce in the center, or to the side. Provide small forks for dipping the oysters in the sauce.

BUCKWHEAT BLINIS WITH CAVIAR SOUR CREAM SAUCE AND SALMON ROE

This recipe must be started a day in advance, as the blini batter must be refrigerated overnight.

Serves: 12

INGREDIENTS

Buckwheat Blinis

½ cup buckwheat flour
¼ cup + 2 tbsps white all-purpose flour
½ tsp salt
1 cup whole milk
½ package active dry yeast
1 egg, separated
Olive oil for frying

Caviar Sour Cream Sauce

3 tbsps caviar, preferably Oscietre
½ cup sour cream
1 tsp lime juice
Freshly ground black pepper

5 tbsps salmon roe, to garnish
12 dill sprigs, to garnish

METHOD

To prepare the blini batter, sift the two flours and the salt together in a medium-sized mixing bowl. In a small saucepan, warm the milk over a low heat until tepid and then stir in the yeast with a spoon. Once the yeast has completely dissolved, whisk in the egg yolk and add the mixture to the sifted flours. Continue whisking until you have a thick batter free of any lumps. Cover the bowl and refrigerate overnight. The next day, allow the batter to come to room temperature. Once at room temperature, beat the egg white until stiff, then fold gently into the batter until well incorporated. This may be done up to one hour in advance and left at room temperature.

To cook the blinis, heat 1 tbsp olive oil over a medium heat in a medium-sized non-stick skillet for about 2 minutes until hot. Use about 2 tbsps batter to form little 2-inch pancakes and cook in batches of 4. Cook for about 1½ minutes, until tiny holes begin to appear on the surface and the bottom is nicely browned. Then flip the pancakes over using a spatula and continue to cook for about 1 minute until the other side is also nicely browned and cooked through. Place the cooked blinis on a cutting board, wipe the pan with a paper towel, add a further 1 tbsp olive oil if necessary and continue cooking the blinis in this way until the batter has been used up. Using a 1½-inch cookie cutter, cut the cooked blinis into neat rounds. Once shaped, place on a plate and cover with plastic wrap to prevent them drying out. When all the blinis have been cooked, set them aside at room temperature, loosely covered.

Prepare the caviar sour cream sauce by combining all the ingredients in a small bowl and mixing gently with a spoon until just blended. Refrigerate if not serving immediately. The sauce may be prepared up to 1 hour in advance.

Just before serving, arrange the blinis on a serving platter and then spoon about ½ tsp of the caviar sour cream sauce into the center of each one. Top with a little salmon roe and a sprig of dill. Serve immediately.

CEVICHE OF SCALLOPS WITH LIME, CILANTRO AND OLIVE OIL

This dish should be started several hours in advance and kept refrigerated.

Serves: 12

INGREDIENTS

About 10oz fresh sea scallops
¼ cup lime juice
6 whole cilantro sprigs for the marinade

3 tbsps extra-virgin olive oil
½ cup tomato flesh, cut in ¼-inch dice
3 tbsps finely chopped cilantro leaves
2 tbsps finely chopped chives
Fine sea salt and freshly ground pepper to taste

METHOD

Remove the tough muscle on the side of the scallops and rinse them well under cold running water. Drain the scallops and pat dry. Using a sharp, thin-bladed knife, slice them into ¼-inch slices. Next, cut these slices into ¼-inch dice and place in a medium-sized mixing bowl. Once all the scallops are diced, add the lime juice, the whole cilantro sprigs and the olive oil to the bowl. Mix gently and refrigerate for a minimum of 3 and a maximum of 6 hours. Just before serving, drain off any excess juices and mix in the diced tomato flesh, and chopped herbs, and season to taste with salt and pepper. Serve on small plates or in small singing scallop shells.

Three of Washington's major sights: the Lincoln Memorial, the Washington Monument and the dome of the Capitol.

· Mrs. Steuart Martens ·

Cathy Martens is another Washington Hostess who works full-time at what she used to do as a volunteer. She is an events planner with Georgetown Design Group, specializing in large-scale productions like major fashion shows. Cathy, her husband Steuart, an automobile dealer, and their two young sons live in a traditional brick colonial which is often bedecked with homemade holiday decorations. At Halloween, for example, she and the boys make scarecrows and decorate pumpkins and ghosts. She is equally imaginative about table decorations. A collection of Herend china in the rust pattern inspires different arrangements; sometimes Cathy creates a miniature forest with flowers, trees, rocks and her Herend animals.

A native Californian, she sees her entertaining as definitely reflecting her home state – the sun porch is bright and cheerful, with wicker furniture and pink lillies on fabric and hand painted border; her menus use lots of fresh vegetables and fresh fruit. Cathy volunteers her time with groups that deal primarily with children: the Capital Children's Museum; Second Genesis, a long-term drug rehabilitation program; and Davis Memorial Goodwill Industries, which offers vocational rehabilitation for socially and physically disabled people.

Small, elegant snacks (above) go well with pre-dinner drinks without spoiling the appetite. Facing page: Sonoma Salad.

SONOMA SALAD

Serves: 8

INGREDIENTS

Citrus Vinaigrette

$^3/_4$ cup olive oil
$^1/_4$ cup cider vinegar
Freshly squeezed juice of 1 orange, 1 lime and 1 lemon
Salt and white pepper to taste

1 bunch watercress
3 bunches mâche
1 head baby red oak leaf lettuce
$^1/_4$ lb spinach
1 head bibb lettuce
16 orange segments
1 cup almond slivers
1 avocado, sliced
1 lime, sliced

METHOD

Combine all the ingredients for the citrus vinaigrette in a bowl. Blend well, adjust seasoning and chill until required.

Cut and wash all the salad leaves thoroughly. Drain. Arrange the salad leaves on 8 plates and decorate with the orange segments, almond slivers, and slices of avocado and lime. Dress each plate of salad with 1oz of citrus vinaigrette.

GRILLED LOBSTER MEDALLIONS IN A POOL OF RED AND YELLOW PEPPER COULIS STUDDED WITH NEW WORLD CORN

Serves: 8 people

INGREDIENTS

3 red peppers
3 yellow peppers
2 pints heavy cream
Salt and pepper
Curry powder (optional)

8 4oz lobster tails
$^1/_2$ cup white kernel corn
Rosemary

METHOD

First prepare the red and yellow pepper coulis. Core and seed the peppers and chop coarsely. Divide the cream between two saucepans and place the red peppers in one and the yellow peppers in the other. Season both to taste and simmer for 25 minutes over a low heat. In a processor, blend each separately until smooth and chill the two coulis until required.

Remove the lobster tails from their shells and place a bamboo skewer through each, to prevent the tails curling when cooked. Grill the lobster tails over mesquite, turning frequently. Once cooked, allow to cool before refrigerating until required.

To serve, divide the two coulis between 8 plates, placing the red pepper sauce on the left of each plate and the yellow pepper on the right. They should run together in the middle. Using a knife, swirl the two sauces together, creating a web of streaks. Slice each lobster tail into medallions and arrange in the center of the plate. Garnish the right-hand side of the plates with rosemary and the left-hand side with corn kernels.

MESQUITE GRILLED VEAL CHOPS

Serves: 8

INGREDIENTS

8 10oz veal loin chops
$^1/_2$ cup oil
Salt and pepper to taste

METHOD

Brush the veal chops with oil to prevent them sticking to the grill. Season each chop. Grill the chops over mesquite, turning so they cook equally on each side, until done.

PLUM AND JACK DANIELS SAUCE

Yield: 1 quart

Right: Grilled Lobster Medallions in a Pool of Red and Yellow Pepper Coulis Studded with New World Corn.

INGREDIENTS

1 quart veal stock
2 oz Jack Daniels bourbon
½ cup hoisin sauce
½ cup cornstarch
Salt and pepper to taste

METHOD

In a saucepan, combine the veal stock, bourbon and hoisin sauce and simmer for 30 minutes.

Mix the cornstarch with ½ cup cold water and add to the sauce, stirring continuously until it thickens. Season to taste.

POTATO AND MAUI ONION CAKE

Serves: 8

INGREDIENTS

3lbs potatoes, peeled and cut into ¼-inch dice
1 maui onion, finely diced
4 eggs
1 pint heavy cream
2 tsps salt
1 tsp white pepper
½ tsp nutmeg

METHOD

Cook the diced potatoes for 8-10 minutes in boiling water. Drain and mix the potatoes with the diced onion. In a separate bowl, mix together the eggs, heavy cream and seasonings. Combine this mixture with the potatoes and onion.

Place the mixture in 8 greased individual soufflé dishes. Bake in a water bath for 1 hour in a preheated 300° oven. Allow to rest for 15 minutes before turning out onto plates.

MELANGE OF SUGAR SNAP PEAS AND BABY CARROTS

Serves: 8

INGREDIENTS

1 gallon water
3lbs sugar snap peas, stems removed
60 baby carrots, peeled and washed
Salt and white pepper to taste

METHOD

Bring the water to a boil and place in the sugar snap peas. Cook for approximately 4 minutes. Be careful not to overcook the peas, they should still be al dente.

Place the baby carrots in cold water to cover and bring to a boil, cooking until al dente.

Mix with the cooked sugar snap peas, season to taste and serve.

POACHED PEARS FILLED WITH CHOCOLATE GANACHE AND RASPBERRIES AND SERVED WITH RASPBERRY COULIS AND CRÈME ANGLAIS

Serves: 8

INGREDIENTS

8 pears
1 gallon water
1lb sugar
1 tsp cinnamon
1 tsp nutmeg

Ganache with Raspberries

6oz sweet chocolate
2oz heavy cream
1 cup fresh raspberries

Facing page: Mesquite Grilled Veal Chops accompanied by Melange of Sugar Snap Peas and Baby Carrots, Potato and Maui Onion Cake, and Plum and Jack Daniels Sauce.

Above and left: Poached Pears filled with Chocolate Ganache and Raspberries and Served with Raspberry Coulis and Crème Anglais.

Creme Anglais

1 pint heavy cream
1 egg yolk
½ lb sugar
1oz vanilla extract

Raspberry coulis

8oz raspberry preserves
2oz corn syrup
2oz Chambord

METHOD

Peel and core the pears. Dissolve the 1lb sugar in the water over a gentle heat, stirring continuously. Bring to the boil, then add the cinnamon and nutmeg. Poach the pears in this syrup until just tender. Lift the pears out of the syrup and allow to cool.

To make the ganache, melt the chocolate in a double boiler and add the cream. Allow to cool to body temperature and then gently mix in the raspberries. Use this mixture to stuff the cooled pears. Chill.

Make the créme anglais by bringing the cream to a boil with ¼lb of the sugar. In a bowl, combine the remaining ¼lb sugar, the egg yolk and the vanilla extract. Add this to the hot cream mixture slowly, stirring continuously. Return to the stove and continue stirring until the sauce coats the back of the spoon. Allow to cool and then chill.

Finally, prepare the raspberry coulis. Melt the preserves in a saucepan and add the corn syrup and Chambord, mixing well. Allow to cool and then chill.

To serve, divide the créme anglais and the raspberry coulis between 8 serving plates, putting one on the right of each plate and one on the left. Swirl together gently and place a stuffed pear in the center.

A peaceful scene along the towpath of the Chesapeake and Ohio Canal in Georgetown.

· MRS. ROBERT FOLEY ·

Both Carol Foley and her husband Bob, a developer-builder, are from families that go back several generations in Washington. They love to entertain and their home is ideal, with lots of space for children, friends and dogs, a pretty garden and swimming pool. When Carol gives a formal, seated dinner, she likes to prop a menu next to the place card for each guest. "People appreciate knowing what wines they are drinking and also it's a souvenir of the evening." Carol serves on the board of the National Symphony Orchestra and Meridian House International, and has chaired balls for both as well. She made a special contribution to Washington eight years ago when she and a friend started Entertaining People, a major fund-raising event that showcases rooms designed by well-known decorators from here and around the country, each designed for a different celebrity. Her table here is set for a late supper party after the fall opening of the National Symphony, and the setting for this evening is designed around an unusual set of a rare old Meissen Monkey Band.

CHEDDAR STICKS

Makes: 10 servings

INGREDIENTS

1 loaf salt-rising bread
1lb unsalted butter
8oz sharp Cheddar cheese, grated
Sesame seeds

METHOD

Remove the crusts from the loaf and cut the bread into strips. Melt the butter, a stick at a time, in a small saucepan. Soak the bread sticks in the melted butter and then roll in the cheese. Place on greased cookie sheets and sprinkle with sesame seeds. Bake in a preheated 400° oven for 10 minutes, or until toasted.

PALM BEACH MUSTARD SAUCE

Makes: about 3½ cups

INGREDIENTS

2 cups mayonnaise
1 cup sour cream
2 tbsps Worcestershire sauce
½ cup Pommery mustard
Dash Tabasco sauce
Salt and black pepper to taste

An elegantly arranged cold table, with caviar, shrimp, oysters and ice-cold vodka, allows guests to help themselves to hors d'oeuvres.

METHOD

Combine all the ingredients in a bowl, mixing together well and seasoning to taste. Store in a plastic container and refrigerate until required.

BROCCOLI PURÉE

Serves: 4

INGREDIENTS

2 bunches broccoli
1 1/2 gallons boiling salted water
2 tbsps butter
1/4 cup heavy cream
Salt and white pepper to taste

METHOD

Separate the broccoli flowerets from the stems. Using a vegetable peeler, peel the stems and then cut them into 1/2-inch pieces. Cook both stems and flowerets in the boiling water until fork tender. Drain and place in a mixer. Blend until smooth. Add the butter and cream and blend smooth again. Season with salt and pepper to taste.

Above: chilled caviar and vodka – the ideal combination.

RISOTTO WITH WILD MUSHROOMS

Serves: 6

INGREDIENTS

2 tbsps butter
1 cup wild mushrooms
1/2 cup onion, finely diced
1 cup raw Persian rice
2 cups chicken stock
Salt
Black pepper

METHOD

In a saucepan, melt the butter and add the mushrooms and onion, cooking until the onion is translucent. Add the rice and toss with the vegetables until well coated. Stir in the chicken stock, cover and simmer for 20 minutes. Season to taste with salt and pepper and serve immediately.

Right: Winter Squash Purée, Broccoli Purée and Risotto with Wild Mushrooms pictured with succulent ribs of beef.

Maestro Rostropovich

Mæstro Rostropovich

Left: a spectacular centerpiece on a musical theme suits a supper party following the fall opening of the National Symphony Orchestra.

WINTER SQUASH PURÉE

Serves: 6

INGREDIENTS

3 butternut squash
1 1/2 gallons boiling salted water
2 tbsps butter
1/2 cup heavy cream
1 tsp cinnamon
1 tsp nutmeg
Salt and white pepper to taste

METHOD

Peel and seed the squash. Dice the flesh into 1/2-inch squares. Cook in the boiling salted water until fork tender. Drain and then blend in a mixer with the butter and cream, until smooth. Stir the cinnamon and nutmeg into the purée and season to taste with salt and pepper.

SPICED PECANS

INGREDIENTS

2 egg whites
4 tbsps cold water
1 cup sugar
1/4 cup cornstarch
1 1/4 tbsps cinnamon
1 tsp ginger
1/2 tsp nutmeg
1/4 tsp salt
1 tsp allspice
9oz pecan halves

METHOD

Combine the egg whites with the water and then beat in all the remaining ingredients, except the pecan halves, mixing thoroughly. Dip the nuts individually into this mixture. Bake on foil-lined cookie sheets in a preheated 250° oven for 1 hour. Allow to cool before storing in a covered container.

CONCERTO WAFERS

Makes: 3 dozen

INGREDIENTS

4 cups all-purpose flour
1 tsp baking powder
½ tsp salt
4 eggs
2 cups granulated sugar
1 tsp lemon zest
Anise seeds

METHOD

Sift together the flour, baking powder and salt. Place the eggs, sugar, and lemon zest in the bowl of an electric mixer and beat about 3 minutes on medium speed. Beat in the flour ½ a cup at a time. Cover the dough and chill.

Roll out the dough with a floured rolling pin. Cut into violin shapes. Sprinkle anise seeds over a baking sheet. Place the wafers on the sheet and allow to rest for 2 hours. Bake in a preheated 325° oven for 15 minutes.

Carol Foley believes in placing a menu beside each place setting so that each guest knows exactly what is being served.

The Memorial Museum within the George Washington Masonic National Monument.

· Washington Hostess Cookbook ·

· MRS. FRITZ-ALAN KORTH ·

Penne Percy Korth was appointed by President George Bush as Ambassador to Mauritius, the Indian Ocean island nation. After serving the three-year appointment, she and her husband Fritz-Alan, an attorney, will be returning to Washington. Both the Korths are Texans and longtime Bush friends. Penne began volunteering for George Bush in 1964 in his first senate campaign. She was co-chairman of the American Bicentennial Presidential Inaugural, a $25-million celebration. Before being named ambassador, Penne was Washington senior associate with Sotheby's, the international art auction house, in their trust and estate division. The perfect service for an outdoor dinner by the Korths' pool is the china specially produced for the Bush inaugural. Even when working for Sotheby's, Penne was an indefatigable volunteer for, among other causes, the Diplomatic Council of the Friends of Art and Preservation in Embassies, the International Neighbors Club III, and the National Museum of Women in the Arts.

Crab Pâté

Makes: 1 3lb mold

Ingredients

1oz shallots, cut into 1/4-inch dice
1 cup dry white wine
1oz butter
1 1/2 lbs sole fillet
1/4 cup fresh lemon juice
1 1/4 lbs crabmeat
4-5 egg whites
Heavy cream (see below)
Salt
White pepper
Cayenne pepper
Fresh lemon juice
8oz celery, blanched and finely diced
1/2 cup dill , finely chopped
4oz carrots, blanched and finely diced
Savory cabbage leaves, blanched and drained
Crabmeat
Egg white
Fish stock
Fresh dill sprigs and aspic, to garnish

Method

Sauté the shallots in the white wine and butter until transparent. Leave to cool in the liquid. Marinate the sole and the cooled shallot mixture in the lemon juice overnight. Drain. Weigh when done.

Clean the crabmeat and remove any cartilage. Separate the larger from the smaller pieces. Put the large pieces aside. Place the small pieces and the drained fish in a fine meat grinder and run through once only. Transfer to a Robot-Coupe, add 4-5 egg whites and 10-15% of the

From right: Baby Veal Loin, Crab Pâté, Horseradish Velouté and Corn Pudding – mouthwatering fare for a poolside meal.

MOËT
MOËT & CHANDON

total weight of the ground mixture in heavy cream. Add salt, white pepper, cayenne and fresh lemon juice to taste. If this farce mixture is too thick, thin with a little of the juices from the sole marinade. Refrigerate. Whip another 10-15% of the total weight of the ground mixture in heavy cream and fold into the farce. Add the drained diced celery, chopped dill and the large pieces of crabmeat. Refrigerate.

Add the diced carrot to ¾lb of the farce mixture in a separate bowl. Lay out a piece of foil the length of your mold and line the foil with plastic wrap. Place the blanched savory cabbage leaves over the plastic wrap to cover. Spread the ¾lb farce onto the cabbage to an even ¼ inch. Dip the extra crabmeat lightly in the egg white to coat. Place the crabmeat onto the middle of the farce. Roll like a pinwheel, closing the ends tightly. Blanch in the fish stock until 120° then allow to cool completely. Line a mold with plastic wrap and place ⅓ of the remaining farce in the bottom. Place the cooled seafood sausage in the middle and cover completely with the balance of the farce. Cover the mold with foil. Line a deep baking pan with cardboard, fill one third full with water, stand the mold on the cardboard and bake in a preheated 225°-230° oven for 1¼ hours, or until 115°-120° in the center. Take the pâté mold out, allow to cool and then refrigerate overnight. To serve, turn pâté out, garnish the top with the dill sprigs and brush it lightly with aspic.

Bed for Crab Pâté

1lb dried black-eyed peas, soaked overnight
3 cups carrots, julienned
3 cups leeks, julienned
3 cups celery root, julienned

Cook the black-eyed peas in chicken stock with bay leaves and pepper until tender. Cool and then chill. Lightly blanch the vegetables. Mix all the ingredients together with a light vinaigrette before serving and use as a bed for the above dish.

BABY VEAL LOIN

Serves: 10

INGREDIENTS

3½ lbs boneless saddle of veal, tenderloin removed
Salt and pepper, to season meat
1½ cups chopped onion
1 cup chopped celery
⅜ cup (3oz) butter
¼ cup mushrooms
2 cloves garlic, minced
1 bay leaf
1 tbsp rubbed sage
1 tsp ground rosemary
2 tsps salt
2 tsps ground black pepper
4 cups croutons
½ cup white wine
Horseradish Velouté (see separate recipe)

METHOD

To prepare the loin, trim away the cartilage and any large pieces of fat. Butterfly the loin so that the piece of meat lies flat. Season the meat with salt and pepper and refrigerate.

To prepare the stuffing, sauté the onion and celery in the butter until transparent. Add the mushrooms, garlic, bay leaf and the remaining seasonings and sauté 2 minutes more. Add the croutons and the wine and sauté for another 2 minutes. Remove from the heat. Fold all the ingredients together, making sure all the liquid is incorporated. Refrigerate until cool.

To roll the veal, place the stuffing in the middle of the meat and fold the saddle over, rolling until the stuffing is encased. Cover each end of the roll with aluminum foil. Tie up with butcher's twine. Start to roast in a preheated 425° oven. Brown on all sides for 15 minutes. Turn the oven down to 350° and finish cooking for 1¼ hours.

The stuffed veal saddle can be sliced into a minimum of 22 slices and garnished as desired. Serve with Horseradish Velouté.

HORSERADISH VELOUTÉ

Makes: about 1 cup

INGREDIENTS

¼ cup diced onions
4 fresh mushrooms, quartered
¼ cup Madeira wine
½ cup demi glace (reduced rich beef stock)
1 cup whipping cream
5 tbsps horseradish, or to taste
Salt and pepper to taste

Patriotic colors and china specially produced for President Bush's inauguration are a feature of Penne Korth's outdoor dinner.

METHOD

Lightly degrease the roasting pan from the Baby Veal Loin recipe. Add the onion, and mushrooms and sauté until golden brown. Deglaze with the Madeira wine and reduce until almost dry. Add the demi glace and cream, and reduce until of sauce consistency. Remove from the heat. Add the horseradish, and salt and pepper to taste. Strain the sauce and keep it warm in a bain marie, or put in a covered container over hot water.

CORN PUDDING

Serves: 6

INGREDIENTS

4 strips bacon
¾ cup chopped onion
1 bell pepper, diced
1 cup milk
1 cup cream
2 tbsps butter
3 eggs
1 cup white corn kernels
2 tbsps + 2 tsps flour
Salt and white pepper to taste
½ tsp thyme
1½ tbsps chopped parsley

METHOD

Cut the bacon into small pieces and fry until crisp. Remove from the pan and sauté the onion in the fat until transparent. Add the bell pepper and cook for 3 minutes.

Heat the milk and cream over a low heat until warm. Add the butter, cooking until melted. Beat the eggs and add the milk mixture, corn, flour, salt, herbs, bacon, onion and pepper.

Pour the mixture into an ungreased 1½-quart oval baking dish and bake in a preheated 350° oven for 1¼ hours, until golden brown.

APPLE-CRANBERRY BROWN BETTY

Serves: 10

INGREDIENTS

Butter and sugar for sprinkling soufflé dish
10 Granny Smith apples
1 tsp lemon juice
6 tbsps clarified butter
3 tbsps sugar
2 cups cranberries, washed and dried
1 cup golden raisins, soaked in warm water for 15 minutes and squeezed dry
Zest of 2 oranges
1 cup light brown sugar
¼ tsp mace
1 tsp ground cinnamon
3 cups bread crumbs made from 2-day-old white bread, crusts removed
½ cup melted butter
Bourbon Custard Sauce (see separate recipe)

Butter a 2-quart straight-sided glass soufflé dish and sprinkle with sugar.

METHOD

Peel, core and quarter the apples. Cut each quarter crosswise into thirds and reserve. Sprinkle the lemon juice over the apples. Heat 2 tbsps of the clarified butter in a large frying pan and add 1/3 of the apple pieces. Sprinkle with 1 tbsp of the sugar and sauté the apples over a high heat until lightly caramelized. Remove the apples and reserve in a bowl. Repeat this process until all the apples have been sautéed. Add the next 6 ingredients to the apples and mix well.

Mix the bread crumbs with the melted butter. Line the bottom of the soufflé dish with 1/3 of the bread crumb mixture. Top with 1/2 the apple-cranberry mixture, then repeat the layers, finishing with the remaining bread crumbs. Bake in a preheated 375° oven for 1 1/4-1 1/2 hours. Serve with lemon or vanilla ice cream and Bourbon Custard Sauce.

Bourbon Custard Sauce

Makes: about 2 cups

INGREDIENTS

2 cups milk, scalded
5 tbsps sugar
Pinch salt
4 egg yolks, lightly beaten
1 tsp vanilla extract
1 tbsp bourbon whiskey

METHOD

Heat the milk, sugar and salt in the top of a double boiler over a moderate heat, stirring until the sugar has dissolved. Spoon a little of the hot, sweet milk onto the egg yolks. Return this to the pan, set over simmering water, and cook, stirring constantly, for 6-10 minutes until thickened and no raw egg taste remains. Mix in the vanilla extract and bourbon and serve with the Apple-Cranberry Brown Betty.

Right: Apple-Cranberry Brown Betty.

CHANDON
PEACE
PLENTY
AND
INDEPENDENCE

The ornate Renaissance splendor of the Great Hall of the Library of Congress.

·Washington Hostess Cookbook·

·Mrs. Richard Berendzen·

In the ten years her husband, Richard, has been president of The American University, Gail Berendzen's social calendar has been the school one. When life on this 12,000-student campus in Washington, D.C., resumes in August, Gail becomes a nonstop whirlwind until classes let out in May. Her entertaining is more varied than that of most hostesses: an average of two events a week at the 1930's Georgian stucco house near the campus bring in faculty for breakfast meetings, students for special programs and recognition receptions, board members for luncheons, parents and alumni for teas and brunches, community leaders for buffets, distinguished guests for formal sit-down dinners, and on and on. A series for diplomats' wives called "America and ..." features a professor from the university speaking on topics like "America and Education" or "America and the News Media."

An unflappable hostess, Gail appreciates that people enjoy seeing someone else's home. Off duty, Gail is on the boards of Multiple Sclerosis and Full Circle Dance Theatre, a fledgling dance group, and the Advisor Council for the Samaritans, a suicide prevention hotline. A former teacher, she also participates, as does her husband, in the Mentor Program, a three-year commitment to working with an inner-city teenager. Her hobbies include keeping a diary, something she started at age ten, designing and landscaping fish tanks, and rising at 6 a.m. daily for aerobics class.

OMELET PRIMAVERA

Serves: 4-6

INGREDIENTS

4½ cups egg-eze
6 slices whole grain bread, crusts removed and bread made into crumbs
4oz sliced mushrooms
4oz bean sprouts
1 red pepper, thinly sliced
1 yellow pepper, thinly sliced
4oz snow peas
Fresh basil, chopped
Fresh oregano, chopped

METHOD

Combine the egg-eze and the bread crumbs and blend well. Blanch the vegetables in boiling water for 30 seconds.

Pour the egg mixture into a hot, greased omelet pan and cook until firm. Fill with the blanched vegetables and fold over. Serve the omelet immediately, garnished with the fresh herbs or with a fresh vegetable kebob.

BREAKFAST AMBROSIA

Serves: 4

INGREDIENTS

¼ cup low fat cottage cheese
1 cup plain low fat yogurt
1 tsp rum extract
1 tsp vanilla extract
2 egg whites
2 tbsps fresh orange or tangerine juice
½ cup blueberries
½ cup small strawberries, cleaned and left whole
½ cup ripe mango, diced or sliced
½ cup fresh pineapple, cubed
2 tbsps freshly shredded coconut

METHOD

Combine the cheese, yogurt, and extracts.

In a separate bowl, whip the egg whites with the orange or tangerine juice, until stiff peaks form. Fold into the cheese mixture. Carefully fold in the fresh fruit and top with the shredded coconut. Refrigerate overnight.

The ambrosia may either be served in individual parfait glasses or a large glass bowl.

PUMPKIN DIP

Makes: 8 cups

INGREDIENTS

2 16oz cans pumpkin
2 cups unsweetened apple juice
1 cup unsweetened apple butter
1 cup buckwheat honey
1 tsp pumpkin spice
½ tsp nutmeg
½ tsp cinnamon
3½ oz pectin

METHOD

Blend all the ingredients together and boil 1 minute. Allow to cool and then store in the refrigerator.

Serve in a hollowed pumpkin as a spread for bagels, a dip for fruit or a substitute for apple butter.

Facing page: Pumpkin Dip.

Above left: Whole Wheat Blueberry Coffee Cake.
Above: Harvest Grain French Toast.

WHOLE WHEAT BLUEBERRY COFFEE CAKE

Makes: 1 9-inch cake

INGREDIENTS

1 pint blueberries
2½ cups whole wheat flour
3¼ tsps baking powder
1 tsp salt substitute
1½ tsps cinnamon
1 cup lightly toasted wheat germ
6 tbsps light margarine
½ cup honey
½ cup egg-eze
1½ cups low fat milk
2 tsps vanilla extract
2 tsps orange zest

METHOD

Preheat the oven to 375°. Grease a cake pan and sprinkle with a little wheat germ.

Wash and drain the berries. Sprinkle with ½ cup of the flour and allow to sit while you prepare the batter.

Sift together the remaining flour, baking powder, salt substitute, and cinnamon. Add the wheat germ. Cream the margarine and honey, and beat in the egg-eze. Add the milk, vanilla, and orange zest. Add the dry ingredients and stir just enough to mix roughly, then fold in the berries.

Pour the mixture into the prepared pan and bake for 30-35 minutes, or until a toothpick inserted into the middle comes out clean. Turn out onto a rack to cool before serving.

HARVEST GRAIN FRENCH TOAST

Serves: 6

INGREDIENTS

2 cups egg-eze
3 tsps cinnamon
2 tsps nutmeg
4 tsps vanilla extract
2 tsps almond extract
6 1-inch-thick slices 7 grain bread

Topping

3 large Macintosh apples, thinly sliced
2 tbsps light margarine
1 tsp cinnamon

$^1/_2$ tsp nutmeg
2 tsps vanilla extract
4oz non-fat yogurt

METHOD

Combine the egg-eze, cinnamon, nutmeg, and vanilla and almond extracts. Soak the bread slices in this mixture overnight.

Make the topping by sautéing the apples in the margarine with the cinnamon and nutmeg for 5 minutes. Remove from the pan and cool to room temperature. Fold in the yogurt.

On a hot griddle or in a heavy frying pan, cook the soaked bread slices on both sides until golden brown. Serve the toast topped with the apple mixture.

OAT BRAN CRUSTED BREAKFAST PIE

Makes: 1 10-inch pie

INGREDIENTS

Crust

2 cups oat bran
$^3/_4$ cup ground cheerios
$^3/_4$ cup egg-eze
$^1/_2$ cup light margarine

Oat Bran Crusted Breakfast Pie.

Filling 1

2 cups egg-eze
$^{2}/_{3}$ cup low fat, low sodium cheese, grated
$^{2}/_{3}$ cup instant oatmeal
$^{1}/_{4}$ tsp white pepper
$^{1}/_{4}$ cup chopped scallion
1 $^{1}/_{2}$ cups skim milk
$^{3}/_{4}$ cup shredded wheat, lightly toasted

Filling 2

2 cups egg-eze
$^{2}/_{3}$ cup low fat, low sodium cheese, grated
$^{2}/_{3}$ cup instant oatmeal
1 tsp cinnamon
$^{1}/_{2}$ tsp nutmeg
1 $^{1}/_{2}$ cups skim milk
1 $^{1}/_{2}$ tsps vanilla extract
3 thinly sliced apples
$^{3}/_{4}$ cup shredded wheat, lightly toasted

METHOD

Preheat the oven to 350°. Grease and flour a 10-inch French tart pan.

To make the crust, combine all the ingredients well and press the mixture into the prepared pan.

For filling 1, blend the eggs and milk together well, then add the remaining ingredients except the shredded wheat, stirring to combine. Pour the mixture into the prepared crust and top with the shredded wheat.

For filling 2, prepare the egg mixture as before, combining all the ingredients except the apples and shredded wheat. Sauté the apples until just tender and place in the prepared crust, before pouring over the egg mixture. Top with the shredded wheat.

For either filling, bake in the preheated oven for 20-25 minutes, or until set.

FRUIT DIP

Makes: 2 cups

INGREDIENTS

8oz plain yogurt
$^{1}/_{4}$ cup skim milk
$^{1}/_{2}$ tsp sugar substitute
1 tsp grated orange or lemon rind
1 tsp orange or lemon juice
4oz low fat whipped cottage cheese (optional)

Left: Fruit Dip.

METHOD

Blend all the ingredients together and chill. The cottage cheese may be added if a stiffer dip is desired.

To serve, either top with fresh fruit or use as a dip for fresh fruit.

ORANGE SPHERES

Serves: 10

INGREDIENTS

2 tangerines
10 large navel oranges
2 tbsps orange flower water
1 tbsp sugar substitute
¼ tsp grated nutmeg
¼ tsp powdered cinnamon

METHOD

Grate the rind of the tangerines and 2 of the oranges. Combine the grated rind with the remaining ingredients. Peel and cut the oranges into ¼-inch-thick slices. Soak the slices in the orange water mixture overnight.

To serve, arrange the orange slices on a serving platter and dust with a little extra cinnamon and nutmeg.

KIWI LIME MOCKTAIL

Makes: 1 drink

INGREDIENTS

3 kiwi fruit, juiced
1 lime, juiced
Ice
White grape juice to taste

A cornucopia of tempting dishes for a Student Breakfast: Oat Bran Crusted Breakfast Pie, Fruit Dip, Whole Wheat Blueberry Coffee Cake, Orange Spheres, Poached Pears, Omelet Primavera, Kiwi Lime Mocktail, Breakfast Shake and Grilled Breakfast Strips.

METHOD

Combine the juices and strain through cheesecloth.

In a blender, mix the juices with ice until frothy.

Fill a glass half full with white grape juice, then top with the kiwi-lime mixture. Garnish with a mint sprig and a slice of red pear.

GRILLED BREAKFAST STRIPS

Serves: 4

INGREDIENTS

Fresh chopped dill, to taste
3 tbsps plain low fat yogurt
1 clove garlic, minced, or 1 chopped shallot
¼ cup cucumber, puréed
2 6oz boneless chicken breasts, skinned

METHOD

Combine the dill, yogurt, garlic, and cucumber together thoroughly.

Cut the chicken into 1-inch strips, and marinate in the dill-yogurt mixture overnight.

Cook the chicken on a very hot griddle or in a heavy frying pan until tender.

POACHED PEARS

Serves: 4

INGREDIENTS

4 ripe pears
1 3oz package unsweetened raspberry gelatin
½ cup boiling water
3 cinnamon sticks
1 cup tawny port wine
Cloves, cinnamon, and nutmeg to garnish

METHOD

Preheat the oven to 350°.

Carefully peel, halve, and core the pears. Place them in a shallow baking pan, flat side up. Combine the boiling water and gelatin and allow it to dissolve, then add the remaining ingredients. Pour this over the pears.

Bake the pears for 15 minutes, basting often with the gelatin mixture. Turn the pears and continue to bake another 15 minutes. Serve the pears either hot or cold, sprinkled with the powdered spices.

BREAKFAST SHAKE

Makes: 8 drinks

INGREDIENTS

1 cup skim milk
1 cup fresh orange or tangerine juice
1 cup fresh strawberries, raspberries or blackberries
1 cup fresh pineapple
1 small banana
½ tsp rum or coconut extract
1 cup shaved ice

METHOD

Combine all the ingredients in a blender until well mixed. Serve immediately in chilled glasses. Garnish with a sprig of fresh mint or a melon kebob.

HERBED MOZZARELLA AND ROASTED PEPPERS

Serves: 8-10

INGREDIENTS

1lb whole-milk mozzarella cheese cut into 1-inch cubes
½ tsp coarsely ground black pepper
1 tsp coarse (Kosher) salt
½ cup extra virgin olive oil
½ tsp oregano
¼ tsp rosemary (optional)
¼ tsp crushed hot pepper

Herbed Mozzarella and Roasted Peppers.

1 tsp thyme (optional)
1 tsp mixed peppers

METHOD

Combine all the ingredients in a medium-sized bowl. Toss to coat the mozzarella evenly. Cover and refrigerate for up to 2 weeks, tossing occasionally. Allow to return to room temperature before using.

SPINACH VEGGIE DIP

Makes: about 4 cups

INGREDIENTS

2 boxes chopped spinach, drained
1 box Knorr vegetable soup mix
2 cups sour cream
1 cup mayonnaise
2 tsps onion flakes
2 tsps fresh dill

METHOD

Combine all the ingredients, mixing together thoroughly, and refrigerate. Prepare the dip 1 day in advance. Allow to return to room temperature and serve in a hollowed out bread loaf. The dip is good with sourdough bread or pumpernickel.

MASCARPONE AND PESTO TERRINE

Makes: 1 terrine

INGREDIENTS

17oz mascarpone
½ cup butter

Pesto

2 cups fresh basil leaves, stripped, coarsely chopped and tightly packed,
or 2 cups fresh flat-leaf Italian parsley, coarsely chopped and 2 tbsps dried basil
1 tsp salt
½ tsp freshly ground black pepper
½ tsps finely chopped garlic
2 tbsps finely chopped pine nuts or walnuts
1-1½ cups olive oil
½ cup freshly grated Sardo, Romano or Parmesan cheese

METHOD

In a food processor blend the mascarpone and butter. Set aside.

To make the pesto, blend the fresh basil, or parsley and dried basil, salt, pepper, garlic, nuts and 1 cup of the olive oil in a blender or food processor at high speed, until smooth, stopping every 5 or 6 seconds to push the herbs down with a rubber spatula. The pesto should be thin enough to run off the spatula easily. If it seems too thick,

A fish in a brandy glass is a novel and effective centerpiece for a buffet table laid with Carrot and Spinach Striped Pâté, Mascarpone and Pesto Terrine, Snow Peas with Lemon-Anchovy Dipping Sauce, Herbed Mozzarella and Roasted Peppers, and Spinach Veggie Dip.

blend in as much as ½ cup more olive oil. Transfer to a bowl and stir in the grated cheese.

Line a terrine with cheesecloth. Spread ⅓ of the mascarpone mixture in the bottom. Layer with ½ the pesto, another ⅓ mascarpone, the remaining pesto and then the remaining mascarpone. Cover and refrigerate overnight.

To serve, unmold onto a serving platter and garnish with fresh basil leaves. Serve with Carr's crackers.

CARROT AND SPINACH STRIPED PÂTÉ

Makes: 1 2-quart mold

INGREDIENTS

½ cup water
2 tbsps light vegetable oil
¼ cup unflavored gelatin
¼ cup whole wheat pastry flour
1 cup milk or reconstituted non-fat dried milk

Carrot Mixture

4 cups sliced carrot
1 tbsp light vegetable oil
½ cup chopped yellow onion
½ tsp finely chopped garlic
2 tsps curry powder
½ tsp chicken flavoring
½ tsp dry mustard
¼ tsp freshly grated nutmeg
Herb or vegetable salt
½ cup pistachio nuts, blanched in salt water and drained (optional)

Spinach Mixture

2lbs fresh spinach, washed and stems left on
1 tbsp light vegetable oil
½ cup yellow onion, chopped
1 tsp garlic, finely chopped
8oz mushrooms, coarsely chopped
1 tsp fresh lemon juice
1 tsp ground cardamom
1 tsp tarragon, finely chopped
1 tsp chervil, finely chopped
Herb or vegetable salt

METHOD

Bring the water and oil to a boil over a medium heat. Remove from heat. Combine the gelatin and flour in a

Right: Carrot and Spinach Striped Terrine.

small bowl and add to the oil and water, stirring until smooth. Blend in the milk. Return to the heat and stir until the mixture comes to a boil and thickens. Freeze until just set, about 7-10 minutes.

Preheat the oven to 325°. Cook the sliced carrot in boiling water until cooked but still crisp. Drain and set aside. Heat 1 tbsp vegetable oil in a large skillet. Add 1/2 cup chopped yellow onion and 1/2 tsp garlic and cook until the onion is translucent. Reduce the heat, add the curry powder and chicken flavoring and cook for 2 minutes, stirring constantly. Transfer the mixture to a food

Snow Peas with Lemon-Anchovy Dipping Sauce.

processor. Add the carrot and purée until smooth. Add 1/3 of the gelatin mixture along with mustard, nutmeg and herb salt to taste and mix well. Mix in the pistachio nuts, if using.

Place the spinach in a large saucepan and sprinkle with water. Cover and cook over a medium heat about 3 minutes. Drain the spinach, place between paper towels and squeeze dry. Blend to a purée in a food processor. Heat 1 tbsp vegetable oil over a medium heat. Add the remaining onion and garlic and cook until the onion is translucent. Increase the heat to high, add the mushrooms and lemon juice and cook 2 minutes. Add the spinach along with the remaining gelatin mixture, the cardamom, tarragon and chervil and purée again. Season with herb salt to taste.

Coat a 2-quart pâté mold or 9x5-inch loaf pan with oil. Spread half the spinach mixture in the bottom. Spread all the carrot mixture carefully over the spinach. Top with the remaining spinach mixture. Cover first with wax paper and then with aluminum foil. Set the mold in a roasting pan and pour in enough hot water to come halfway up the sides of the mold. Bake about 2 hours in the preheated oven. Remove the mold from the pan but do not unwrap. Weight with a heavy object. Let cool to room temperature and then refrigerate for at least 12 hours before serving.

SNOW PEAS WITH LEMON-ANCHOVY DIPPING SAUCE

Makes: about 1½ cups sauce

INGREDIENTS

2 egg yolks
3-4 tbsps Dijon mustard
1 2oz can anchovies, undrained
Juice of 1 lemon, or to taste
1 shallot, chopped
1 cup vegetable oil
¼ cup sour cream (optional)
Salt and freshly ground black pepper
Capers, to garnish (optional)
Snow peas or sugar snaps

METHOD

Combine the egg yolks, mustard, anchovies, lemon juice and shallot in a processor and mix until pale and foamy. With the machine still running, slowly drizzle in the oil, stopping occasionally to make sure the oil is being absorbed. If the sauce is very stiff, thin with sour cream. Season the dip to taste with salt and pepper and stir in a few capers, if desired. Cover and refrigerate until shortly before serving.

String the snow peas or sugar snaps and crisp in iced water. Drain well and arrange in a sunburst pattern on a flat basket. Place the dipping sauce, garnished with capers if desired, in a bowl in the center.

The Old Patent Office Building, with its Great Hall (above), now houses the Smithsonian Institution's National Collection of Fine Arts, the National Portrait Gallery and the Archives of American Art.

·ANIKO GAAL·

Creative and spirited in her work, Aniko Gaal shows the same flair and discriminating taste in her personal lifestyle. "Everyone's so busy," she says, "that if people take the time to come to yet another dinner, the hostess should make the evening memorable and special." It doesn't require a grand gesture, but Aniko's passion is caviar, and when she's giving a special small dinner, she orders caviar from what she considers to be the best caviar shop in the world, in St. Moritz, Switzerland.

A Hungarian-born, Canadian-raised American, Aniko has lived in Europe and South America. Today she travels frequently as Vice President, Fashion and Public Relations for Garfinckel's, a Washington specialty store. Aniko is also a professional painter and her apartment is arranged with an artist's eye. She installed moldings and a faux-fireplace with mantle to counterbalance an 18th-century Swedish painting. She has had seven art exhibits, the last four in Washington showing delicate pen and ink drawings. Some of Aniko's charity work is done through the store which is, she says, very community-minded. Her latest personal fund-raising effort is for the American Associates of Mozarteum Brasileiro, a cultural entity that brings classical music to Brazil.

MINI PALACSINTA WITH CAVIAR

Hungarian "palacsinta", or pancakes, make wonderful hors d'oeuvres served with sour cream and caviar. The best fresh caviar in the world is to be ordered from J. Glattfelder's in St. Moritz, Switzerland; exceptional caviar selection, exceptional service, and exceptional delivery.

Makes: 36-40 1½-2-inch rounds

INGREDIENTS

1 cup flour
1 cup milk
1 tbsp melted, clarified butter
1 heaping tsp sugar
¼ tsp salt
2 eggs
Splash of freshly opened soda

METHOD

Place the above ingredients in a processor, in the order given. Mix for 1 minute and then stop. Scrape the sides with a spatula and mix again, twice, for 15 seconds at a time, making sure the batter is smooth. The finished batter should coat the back of a wooden spoon. Allow to rest for 2 hours.

Melt 1 tsp butter in a non-stick skillet and cook the pancakes over a low heat in batches of eight 1½-2-inch rounds. Cook for 2-3 minutes on each side, or until golden brown. This quantity of batter makes 36-40 1½-2-inch rounds.

When all the batter has been used, arrange the pancakes on a silver platter with an iced bowl of caviar, sour cream and clarified butter.

Right: Mini Palacsinta with Caviar.

SOUPE DE COQUILLES

Serves: 4

INGREDIENTS

Fish Stock

1/4 cup olive oil
1 large onion, chopped
1 clove crushed garlic
3lbs fish heads, tails, spines
1 bottle clam juice (optional)
1 cup white wine
1 leek, washed and sliced
8 parsley sprigs
1/2 bay leaf
1/2 lemon
Salt to taste

1/2 lb bay scallops
1 zucchini, thickly peeled and the peel julienned
1/4 lb snow peas
2 tbsps unsalted butter
Alfalfa sprouts

METHOD

First, make the fish stock. In a large, deep pan, heat the olive oil and, once hot, add the chopped onion and the garlic. Sauté slowly for a few minutes. Add the fish pieces and cook for 3 minutes, stirring frequently, until the fish parts are coated. Add the clam juice, wine, and enough water to cover. Add the rest of the ingredients. Simmer gently for 30 minutes and then strain off the stock. Correct the seasoning with lemon.

In 1 cup of the fish stock, parboil the scallops for 1 minute. Remove the scallops from the stock and set aside. In the same broth, parboil the vegetables for 1 minute. Drain the vegetables and set aside.

Heat 3 cups of the fish stock and place the scallops and vegetables in it. Quickly stir in the butter. Once the scallops and vegetables have heated and cooked through, ladle the soup into serving bowls and garnish with alfalfa sprouts.

ROAST DUCKLING WITH KUMQUATS

Serves: 4

INGREDIENTS

2 duckling
1 tsp salt
1 tsp thyme
3 grindings of pepper
1 medium carrot, cut in half
1 small onion, cut in half

1 1/2 lbs kumquats
3 tbsps sugar
2 quarts water

Brown Stock

Wings, giblets, and necks of 2 ducks
1 small onion
1 clove garlic
1 small carrot
6 parsley sprigs
1/2 bay leaf
Pinch thyme
2 black peppercorns
1 can beef bouillon
Enough water to cover

1/3 cup sugar
1/3 cup red wine vinegar
1 heaping tbsp cornstarch or arrowroot,
mixed to a paste with Dubonnet Grand Marnier

METHOD

Preheat the oven to 450°.

Cut the lower wings off the duckling. Keep for making the stock. Cut and discard all the fat from inside the duckling. Prick the breast, sides, legs, and back of the duckling with a grapefruit knife or any other sharp knife. This allows all the fat to run off during cooking. Dry the duckling very thoroughly inside and out. Season the insides with the salt, thyme, and pepper. Place a halved carrot and onion inside each duckling.

Roast the duckling, breast side up, for 15 minutes. Pour off the fat and lower the heat to 350°. While cooking, rotate the birds every 15 minutes, pouring off the fat with every 1/4 turn. Reserve the brown juices in a separate cup. Turn the duckling breast side up again with the final turn and salt the outside of the breast and back. The duckling

Facing page: Soupe de Coquilles, garnished with alfalfa sprouts.

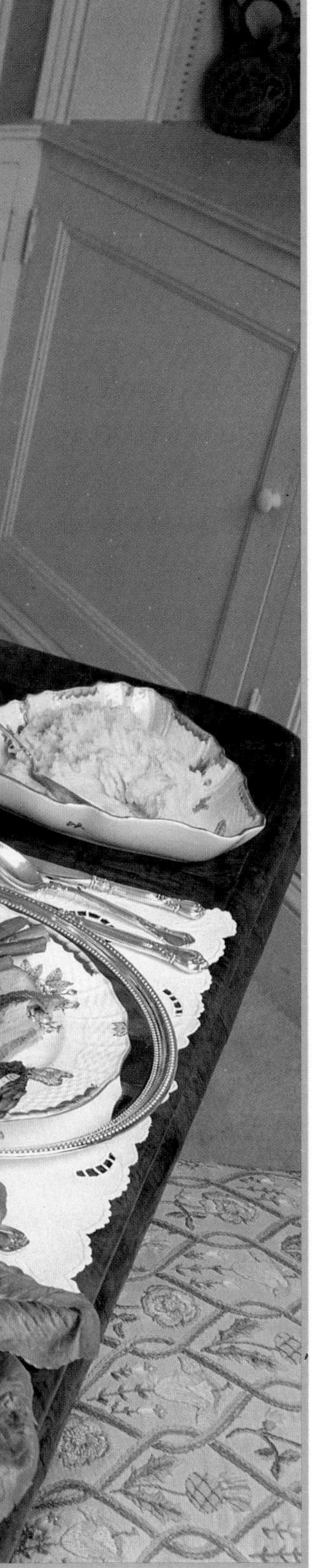

take 1¼ hours to cook. Take out of the oven and allow to cool for 15 minutes before carving.

Meanwhile, boil the kumquats with the 3 tbsps sugar in the 2 quarts water for 3 minutes. Pour off the water, and set aside the kumquats.

To make the brown stock, place all the ingredients in a large saucepan and cook until the meats are ready to fall off the bone. Strain off and reserve the resultant stock.

Prepare the kumquat sauce by boiling the ⅓ cup sugar and the vinegar down to produce a rich mahogany-colored syrup. Remove from the heat and pour in 1 cup of the reserved brown stock, stirring vigorously to dissolve all the syrup. Add the rest of the stock and mix well. Stir in the cornstarch and Dubonnet paste and continue stirring until the sauce has thickened. Stir in half the kumquats. Boil down the reserved brown juices from roasting the duckling with a little Dubonnet to get ½ cup thick duck juices. Add this to the sauce together with 1 tbsp of duck drippings and a few generous splashes of Grand Marnier. Stir in the remaining kumquats. Let the sauce rest for 1 hour, then reheat, correct taste with Grand Marnier, lemon juice and salt and pepper and serve with the roasted ducklings.

PARSNIP PURÉE

Serves: 6

INGREDIENTS

15 parsnips
6-8 chicken cubes
2 potatoes, baked or boiled
½ cup heavy cream
2 tbsps butter
Salt and pepper

METHOD

Peel and quarter the parsnips. In a heavy saucepan, boil the parsnips with the chicken cubes in enough water to cover for about 20 minutes, or until tender. Drain the parsnips and pat dry with paper towels.

Put the parsnips, potatoes, cream, and butter in a processor and blend using the pastry blade until puréed. Season with salt and pepper to taste.

CARROT PURÉE

Make in exactly the same way as above, adding 2 tbsps

Left: Carrot Purée makes a tasty accompaniment to Roast Duckling with Kumquats.

sugar to the cooking water and substituting ½ cup cooked rice for the potatoes. Season the finished purée with freshly grated nutmeg, as well as salt and pepper.

CREMA DE HELADO Y FRAMBUESAS

Serves: 4

INGREDIENTS

4 scoops vanilla ice cream
1 tbsp vanilla extract
1 egg yolk
2 quarts raspberries
Cognac and Grand Marnier
1 tbsp powdered sugar
Well chopped walnuts or chocolate shavings (optional)

METHOD

Over a medium heat, melt the ice cream in a heavy saucepan. Stir frequently, scraping the sides of the pan. Lower the heat. Add the vanilla extract and the egg yolk, stirring vigorously and taking off the heat slightly to prevent the egg coagulating. Once the sauce begins to thicken, continue stirring and add a good dash of Grand Marnier and Cognac.

Divide the cream sauce between 4 dessert plates. Place the raspberries in the middle of the sauce. Sprinkle each serving with powdered sugar, and the walnuts or chocolate shavings, if using.

Crema de Helado y Frambuesas.

The colonnaded Jefferson Memorial.

· Mrs. Jack Coopersmith ·

Esther Coopersmith's interests in politics, international affairs and fund-raising are global in scale and she entertains the same way she operates – mixing diverse groups of power people, friends and artists in serious conversation in a relaxed atmosphere. Esther and her husband Jack, who is in real estate, have a perfect setting for large barbeques in their Potomac, Maryland, home.

Esther's three-page resume leads off with six presidential appointments: she was United States Representative to the United Nations, 1979, and five years later was awarded the United Nations Peace Prize, the first woman recipient since Eleanor Roosevelt. Her international activities focus on the Middle East and the Soviet Union. Among many achievements she initiated, arranged and hosted an afternoon meeting-barbeque for the entire Israeli and Egyptian press during the Camp David Summit, bringing the journalists together for the first time. She is Chairman/Founder of the United States Egyptian Cultural Preservation Committee. She has lectured on campaign skills, fund raising and public relations, participated in national Democratic campaigns, and serves on numerous boards including the Congresswoman's Caucus, the International League for Human Rights and the United Nations Association.

MOP FOR ALL BARBECUE MEATS

Use this to rub over meats or to baste them while they are cooking. Put it on with a little dish mop of the kind that you see in the dime store. As you use it, the flavor will change and improve, for you are constantly transferring smoke and grease from the meat back to the mop concoction. If you have any left over, keep it in the refrigerator.

Makes: about 6 quarts

INGREDIENTS

4 quarts bone stock
3 tbsps salt
3 tbsps dry mustard
2 tbsps garlic powder
1 tbsp ground bay leaf
2 tbsps chili powder
3 tbsps paprika
2 tbsps lu'siana Hot Sauce
2 pints Worcestershire sauce
1 pint vinegar
1 pint oil
3 tbsps MSG or other pep powder

METHOD

Make the bone stock just the way you would start a soup. Buy good stout beef bones from the butcher and boil them. Add all the other ingredients and let stand overnight before using.

DRY RIB SEASONING

This is for sprinkling on spareribs before you barbecue them. Use heaping measures when you are mixing it and do not skimp when using it.

Makes: about 12oz

INGREDIENTS

6 tbsps salt
6 tbsps sugar
1 tbsp dry lemon powder
2 tbsps MSG or other pep powder
2½ tbsps black pepper
1 tbsp paprika

METHOD

Mix all the ingredients together thoroughly and store in a screw-top jar until needed.

DRY POULTRY SEASONING

Sprinkle this on chicken and fowl before barbecuing.

Makes: about 1lb

INGREDIENTS

6 tbsps salt
3 tbsps black pepper
2 tbsps MSG or other pep powder
2 tbsps garlic powder
2 tbsps ground bay leaves
1 tbsp paprika
2 tbsps dry mustard

METHOD

Mix all the ingredients together well and store in a screw-top jar until needed.

BARBECUE SAUCE

Use this as a plate or table sauce with beef, chicken, pork or almost anything else; but don't cook things in it.

The gardens of Esther and Jack Coopersmith's Potomac, Maryland, home provide the perfect setting for barbecues.

Makes: about 2½ cups.

INGREDIENTS

1 cup tomato ketchup
½ cup cider vinegar
1 tsp sugar
1 tsp chili powder
⅛ tsp salt
1½ cups water
3 stalks celery, chopped
3 bay leaves
1 clove garlic
2 tbsps chopped onion
4 tbsps butter
4 tbsps Worcestershire sauce
1 tsp paprika
Dash of black pepper

METHOD

Combine all the ingredients in a saucepan and bring to a boil. Simmer about 15 minutes. Remove from the heat and strain.

Springtime Washington is awash with nature's vivid colors.

Washington Hostess Cookbook

MRS. RAYMOND POSTON

How does the woman who entertains as a business entertain at home? With the same underlying principle: be organized. Gretchen Poston, partner in a multimillion-dollar events planning business, WashingtonInc, and former Social Secretary to the White House, believes that it's a fallacy that one can simply send out invitations and assume that guests will be comfortable. "In order for a guest to be informal and relaxed," she says, "the host has to be almost over-organized. The structure is under ground, but it's there so that guests know what to do." She keeps her guests circulating by using different areas for her favorite dinner party of ten: perhaps the sun porch for cocktails, the dining room (she doesn't like to serve "lap" food), and coffee and liqueur in the drawing room. "I think some sort of welcome is important," she adds. "Just a few words, whether it's a cocktail party or seated dinner."

Gretchen and her husband Raymond, an attorney, live in what she describes as a family house that works well for entertaining because the flow is so good. As a contribution, WashingtonInc is involved in Washington community and business affairs. Gretchen herself works on various charity committees, has recently been a sponsor to the Women's Leadership Summit on Mammography and continues to do work with the Susan G. Komen Foundation.

Crudité Basket with Dill Mayonnaise and Honey Curry Sauce

A wide variety of fresh, lightly blanched vegetables are served to dip into a dill mayonnaise and a honey curry sauce. The selection could include baby carrots, asparagus, endive, fennel, baby golden beets, holland peppers, snow peas, Jerusalem artichokes, miniature squash and yellow tomatoes.

Honey Curry Sauce

Makes: 4 cups

INGREDIENTS

1 quart honey
1/4 cup curry powder
1/2 cup mayonnaise

METHOD

Combine the honey and curry powder in a saucepan. Heat gently until the curry powder has dissolved. Allow to cool. Whisk the mayonnaise into the honey curry mixture and refrigerate until needed.

Dill Mayonnaise

Makes: 4 cups

INGREDIENTS

2 cups mayonnaise
1 cup sour cream
1/2 cup heavy cream
1 tbsp Worcestershire sauce

Right: Crudité Basket with Dill Mayonnaise and Honey Curry Sauce.

1 tbsp brandy
¼ cup white wine
¼ cup finely chopped dill
Salt and pepper to taste

METHOD

Combine all the ingredients, mixing together thoroughly. Refrigerate until needed.

MESQUITE GRILLED RED SNAPPER

INGREDIENTS

Whole red snapper (1½ lbs each)
Fresh herbs
Olive oil

METHOD

Wash the fish and pat dry with paper towels. Stuff the cavity with your choice of fresh herbs.

Prepare a grill with plenty of charcoal and mesquite chips. Cook the fish over the grill, basting frequently with olive oil. Cook for 10 minutes per inch of thickness of fish, until the fish is opaque and flaky.

CANDIED LEMON SLICES

METHOD

Using a sharp serrated bread knife, cut lemons into paper-thin slices; they should be almost transparent. Remove any seeds and discard both ends of the fruit as slices should be of an even size and thickness.

In a large heavy skillet or sauté pan, combine 2 cups granulated sugar and 1 cup water and bring to a rolling boil. Do not stir the syrup mixture or it may become cloudy; shake the pan to help the sugar dissolve. Lower the heat to a simmer once the liquid is clear and bubbling, and add the citrus slices in a single layer. Cook the fruit for 20-40 minutes with the syrup barely simmering. Be careful not to boil the fruit, or the pulp may fall away from the peel and disintegrate.

Mesquite Grilled Red Snapper.

When the fruit slices are cooked and softened, remove them very gently from the syrup with a slotted spoon or flat spatula, and place on a parchment-lined baking sheet to cool.

KUMQUAT ICE CREAM TERRINE

Makes: 1 terrine

METHOD

Line the bottom of a rectangular loaf terrine with a layer of genoise cake.

Spread this with a 1-inch layer of softened kumquat, or any other fruit sorbet and freeze.

Kumquat Ice Cream Terrine, Too Tall Lemon Cake, and Lemon Chess Tart.

Once frozen, cover the sorbet layer with a 1-inch layer of softened vanilla ice cream. Place another layer of genoise cake on top and freeze again.

Repeat the layering of sorbet and ice cream. Wrap the terrine tightly and freeze.

When ready to serve, unmold the terrine onto a serving platter.

LEMON CHESS TART

Makes: 1 8-inch tart

INGREDIENTS

1 8-inch tart shell, partially baked and cooled
4 eggs, lightly beaten
1 cup granulated sugar
1 cup freshly squeezed lemon juice
Grated rind of 2 lemons
¼ cup heavy cream
Candied lemon slices (see separate recipe)

METHOD

Preheat the oven to 375°.

In a bowl, whisk together the eggs, sugar, lemon juice, rind and cream for about 1 minute by hand, until well blended. Pour this mixture into the partially baked tart shell. Gently place the candied lemon slices on the filling, in concentric circles.

Bake for 25-30 minutes, or until the filling is set and the tart and lemon slices are lightly browned on top. Allow to cool before serving.

TOO TALL LEMON CAKE

Makes: 1 9-inch layer cake

INGREDIENTS

Sugar Syrup (makes about 2 cups)
2 cups sugar
¾ cup water
¼ cup strained fresh lemon juice

Genoise Cake Batter
6 whole eggs
¾ cup sugar
¾ cup flour
Few drops lemon extract

Lemon Butter Cream
2 cups sugar
1 cup water
10 egg yolks, beaten
1lb butter, softened
2 tbsps lemon extract

METHOD

First prepare a sugar syrup by stirring the 2 cups sugar and ¾ cup water together in a deep, heavy-based saucepan and cooking over a medium heat until the sugar dissolves. While the syrup is cooking, use a dampened pastry brush to wipe down any stray sugar crystals that cling to the sides of the pan. Once the sugar has dissolved, bring the syrup to a boil and then allow to cool before stirring in the lemon juice.

Place the eggs and the ¾ cup sugar in the top of a double boiler. Set the mixture over warm, not hot, water and beat with a rotary or electric beater until the mixture forms a ribbon. Remove the top pan from the double boiler and continue beating the mixture until it has cooled to room temperature. At this point, sift the flour into the mixture a small quantity at a time, folding it in thoroughly but gently after each addition. Pour the batter into a buttered and floured 9-inch cake pan.

Bake in a preheated 400° oven for 30-35 minutes, or until a tester inserted into the center comes out clean. Turn the cake out immediately onto a wire rack to cool. When it is cold, split it in two horizontally. Flavor ¾ cup of the prepared sugar syrup with a few drops of lemon extract and spoon this over the cut surfaces of the cake.

To make the lemon butter cream, stir the 2 cups sugar and the 1 cup water together in a saucepan set over a medium heat until the sugar dissolves and the liquid comes to a boil. Allow the syrup to boil, without stirring, until it registers 217°-220° on a candy thermometer or reaches the small thread stage.Remove the syrup from the heat. Whisking vigorously, pour the hot syrup onto the egg yolks and continue to beat until the mixture is cool, light and fluffy. Cream the butter until it is very soft, then beat the butter and lemon extract into the yolk mixture until the mixture is shiny and firm enough to spread. Use this rich butter cream to fill and frost the cake.

Over 555 feet high, the Washington Monument is the world's tallest masonry structure.

· Washington Hostess Cookbook ·

· MRS. BILL NELSON ·

Grace Cavert Nelson is the wife of Bill Nelson, Congressman from East Central Florida whose Eleventh District includes the Kennedy Space Center and Disney World. Elected to Congress in 1978, Bill Nelson was Chairman of the Space Subcommittee when he was invited by NASA to fly on the space shuttle *Columbia* in January, 1986. Grace and the Nelsons' children, Billy and Nan Ellen, shared in the training and in the friendships that grew with the *Columbia* crew and their families. Her entertaining reflects two of her interests: space, naturally, and family. "My children," she says, "remain the great joy of my life." Mrs. Nelson has twice visited the severely drought-stricken regions of Africa in order to observe firsthand the plight of starving peeple. She is active in working for those suffering from malnutrition and hunger in Africa and here at home. Other involvements in Washington include the International Club – whose purpose is to promote peace and friendship among women around the world – and the Congressional Wives' Prayer Group. Grace and her college roommate Carol Lascaris designed the interior of the Nelsons' home in McLean, Virginia.

Heart-Shaped Candied Orange Scones

Makes: about 15 scones

Ingredients

1 cup flour
Small pinch of salt
1 tbsp baking powder
¼ stick margarine
¼ cup sugar
⅔ cup milk
¼ cup chopped candied orange

Method

Combine the flour, salt, baking powder and margarine and mix thoroughly until a fine texture is obtained. Make a well in the center and add the sugar, milk and candied oranges. Gradually mix the flour into these ingredients to obtain a firm dough. Roll out to ½-inch thickness and cut into 2-inch wide heart-shaped scones. Brush with egg wash. Let the scones stand for 30 minutes before baking in a preheated 375° oven for 15 minutes.

Coffee Punch

Serves: 50 people

Ingredients

1 gallon strong coffee
½ gallon light cream
1 quart milk
1 gallon vanilla ice cream
1 quart whipped heavy cream
2 cups chocolate shavings
3 tbsps ground cinnamon

Method

Freeze half the coffee in ice cube trays. Mix the frozen and liquid coffee, cream, milk and chopped ice cream together half an hour before serving. Add sugar to taste and top with whipped cream, chocolate shavings, and ground cinnamon.

Chocolate Cups Filled with Key Lime Curd

Makes: 16 cups

Ingredients

Key Lime Curd

2 egg yolks
1 whole egg
⅔ cup granulated sugar
½ cup lime juice
Zest of 7 limes, finely grated

16 chocolate cups, 1 inch in diameter

Method

Place all the ingredients for the key lime curd in a stainless steel bowl, place over a pan of simmering water, and whisk vigorously for at least 10 minutes, or until it becomes fairly thick. Leave to cool and then chill overnight.

Fill each chocolate cup with some of the key lime curd. Decorate with candied violets, angelica or whipped cream.

Facing page: a superb antique silver service graces the sideboard in the McLean, Virginia, home of Grace and Bill Nelson.

PUMPKIN PECAN MUFFINS

Makes: 22 muffins

INGREDIENTS

3 eggs
1 1/2 cups sugar
1/2 cup oil
2 1/2 cups solid pack canned pumpkin
2 3/4 cups flour
Pinch of salt
2 tsps baking soda
1/2 tsp cinnamon
1/2 tsp nutmeg
1/2 tsp cloves
1/2 tsp allspice
2/3 cup chopped pecans

METHOD

Combine the eggs, sugar, oil and pumpkin and mix well. Sift together the flour, salt, baking soda, cinnamon, nutmeg, cloves and allspice. Add the dry ingredients to the pumpkin mixture with the pecans and combine until blended.

Bake in muffin pans in a preheated 350° oven for 35 minutes.

SWAMP CABBAGE AND AVOCADO SALAD WITH ROASTED TOMATO SAUCE

Serves: 4

INGREDIENTS

4oz mâche
1 small can palm hearts
1-2 avocados

Right: designed by Grace Nelson and long-time friend Carol Lascaris, the interior of the Nelson home is the embodiment of good taste. Here, the table is laid with cakes and drinks for a "Southern Mother and Daughter Tea."

$^1/_2$ red pepper, cut in very thin julienne (4 inches x $^1/_8$ inch)
$^1/_2$ yellow bell pepper, cut in very thin julienne as above
8 black olives, halved and pitted
2 ripe tomatoes
1 onion
4 tbsps olive oil
2 tbsps red wine vinegar
6 large basil leaves, chopped
Salt and pepper

METHOD

Arrange the first 6 vegetables attractively in your most beautiful vegetable server. Wash, core and halve the tomatoes.Wash the onion. Leave on 1 layer of brown skin and cut in half. Brush the tomatoes and one half onion with 1 tbsp of the olive oil and allow them to blacken in a preheated 500° oven or on your grill. When done, peel the vegetables and chop them coarsely. Once they have cooled, add the remaining olive oil, red wine vinegar, basil and salt and pepper to taste.

To serve, top the vegetable salad with the sauce.

SATELLITE SNAPPER GARNISHED WITH KEY LIME

Serves: 4

INGREDIENTS

1 cup fish stock
4 5oz boneless baby red snapper fillets, cut into diamond shapes (leave the skin on for color)
2 red peppers, cored, seeded, washed and sliced
$^1/_4$ cup cream
3 tbsps olive oil
4 cloves garlic

The final effect justifies the effort in this "Sunshine Supper" spread featuring Satellite Snapper Garnished with Key Lime masterpiece. Also illustrated are Swamp Cabbage and Avocado Salad with Roasted Tomato Sauce, Indian River Pink Grapefruit Cake, and Palm Coast Lobster with Sea Blue Orange Mint Sauce.

1 cup converted rice
1 1/2 cups water
2 chicken stock cubes
12 saffron threads
2 zucchini, thinly sliced
4 extra long chives, blanched 5 seconds in boiling water
Salt and pepper
1/3 cup pecan pieces, toasted
2 limes

METHOD

Pour the fish stock into an ovenproof pan. Sprinkle the snapper with salt and pepper and place in the stock, skin side up. Cook in a preheated 350° oven until barely done. Remove the fish from the pan and set aside. Add the red pepper to the poaching liquid and cook it until very tender. Add the cream and reduce by half. Remove from the heat and allow to cool. Purée in a food processor or blender and keep warm. Check the seasoning.

Pour the olive oil into a 2-quart ovenproof pot, add the garlic and brown over a high heat. Do not allow the garlic to burn. Add the rice and stir for a few seconds. Stir in the water, chicken cubes, saffron, and salt and pepper. Cook in the preheated 350° oven for 17 minutes.

Wrap the sides of the snapper very carefully with the zucchini slices overlapping each other and tie them securely in place with the chives.

4 minutes before the rice is cooked, place the fish over the rice to allow it to reheat. Spoon the rice onto a serving plate. Plate the fish over and circle the plate with the red pepper sauce. Decorate with the toasted pecan pieces and lime slices and wedges.

PALM COAST LOBSTER WITH SEA BLUE ORANGE MINT SAUCE

Serves: 4

INGREDIENTS

1 1/2 quarts water
1 rib celery
1 onion, peeled
1 small carrot, peeled and cut in half lengthwise
2 bay leaves
4-5 parsley sprigs
1/4 cup vinegar
2 1lb live lobsters
1 tbsp butter
2 tbsps chopped onions
Juice of 2 oranges
Juice of 1 lemon
1 cup heavy cream
1 peppermint branch
3 tbsps blue curaçao
Salt and white pepper
8 mâche leaves
1 bunch tarragon

METHOD

In a shallow 2 1/2-quart pot, bring the water to a boil with the celery, peeled onion, carrot, bay leaves, parsley and vinegar. Cover and simmer for 15 mintues, then plunge the lobsters into the stock and cook for 8 minutes. Remove the lobsters from the liquid and allow to cool completely.

Meanwhile, melt the butter in a saucepan over a low heat and cook the chopped onion until just tender. Pour over 2 cups of the lobster stock and reduce by two thirds. Add the orange and lemon juice, and reduce by half. Add the cream and peppermint and reduce again by half. Strain the sauce through a fine sieve and, when completely cool, add the blue curaçao.

Remove the meat from the claws and tails, being careful to keep the pieces intact. Slice each tail into 4 medallions.

Divide the sauce between 4 serving plates, spreading it out in a pool. Place 1 claw and 2 medallions in each pool of sauce. Decorate with the mâche and the tarragon.

INDIAN RIVER PINK GRAPEFRUIT CAKE

Makes: 1 9-inch layer cake

INGREDIENTS

3 eggs
1/8 tsp cream of tartar
1/8 tsp salt
1/2 cup sugar
1/2 cup flour

Custard

1 cup milk
3 egg yolks
1/3 cup sugar
2 tbsps flour

5 ruby grapefruit
1/4 cup Grand Marnier or Cointreau
1/4 cup apricot marmalade
1 cup chopped pistachios
Candied violets and candied orange peel, to decorate

METHOD

Preheat the oven to 350°. Separate the 3 eggs and beat the yolks until they are creamy and light colored. Beat the egg whites in a separate bowl. After a few minutes, add the cream of tartar and the salt and continue beating until stiff. Beat in the 1/2 cup sugar. Fold first the beaten egg yolks and then the 1/2 cup flour into the egg white mixture. Pour the batter into a buttered and floured 9-inch cake pan and bake about 40 minutes in the preheated oven. Turn out onto a rack and allow to cool.

To make the custard, bring the milk to a boil over a low heat. In a separated bowl work the egg yolks and sugar together until a ribbon is formed and then work in the flour. Pour a quarter of the boiling milk onto the egg mixture and then pour this back into the remainder of the milk in the saucepan. Mix well and cook over a low heat until the custard boils. Set aside to cool and then chill.

Over a glass bowl, peel the grapefruit using a sharp serrated knife. Begin by cutting off the ends and then follow the contour of the grapefruit. Reserve all the juices which collect in the bowl. Cut down either side of the membrane that divides each grapefruit section and take out the section. Place the sections in a separate bowl. Squeeze the juice from the membranes into the glass bowl and add the Grand Marnier or Cointreau.

Cut the cake horizontally into 3 equal layers. With a pastry brush, dampen each layer of the cake with the flavored grapefruit juice. Spread a 1/4-inch-thick layer of custard over the first layer. Top with the second layer and repeat the operation. Spread the remaining custard around the sides of the cake and arrange the grapefruit sections in a spiral pattern on top. Melt the apricot marmalade with 3 tbsps water over a low heat. Meanwhile, coat the sides of the cake evenly with the chopped pistachios. Brush the marmalade over the grapefruit sections and keep very cold until serving. Decorate with a few candied violets or candied orange peel before serving.

Above: the coffered dome within the colonnaded Statuary Hall in the Capitol.

·Washington Hostess Cookbook·

·Mrs. Frank Ikard·

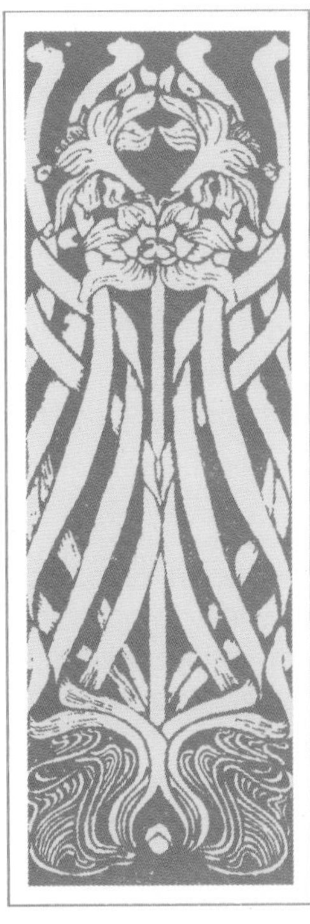

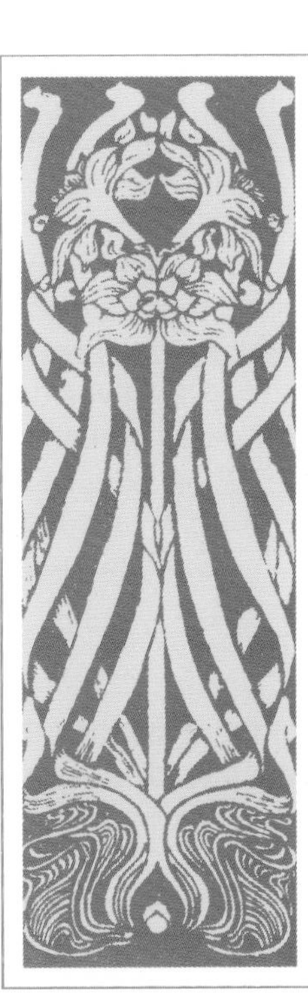

Jayne Ikard and husband Frank have hosted clam bakes, barbeques, black-tie dinners (these mostly), buffet dinners, Sunday brunches and suppers, everything *except* cocktail parties, which neither finds a satisfactory form of getting together with friends. They've done seated dinners with Jamaican food, Italian food and Japanese food. But the Ikards' favorite dishes, like the recipes here, are what she calls "melting pot" foods, an American mix of old-timers. Jayne prefers small groups of friends in an informal atmosphere, with guests serving themselves out of the kitchen. "Eight is the best number," she says, "or three tables of six. That way you can have some real conversation, with everyone participating and contributing." The first woman bureau chief for *Newsweek*, Jayne is a columnist and radio and television commentator with a specialty in "politics of the domestic variety." She is a Bostonian by birth and Texan by marriage – Frank is a former judge and congressman from Texas and is now chairman of the board of Institutional Communications Corporation. Jayne is the only woman named "Y Guy of the Year," for her contribution to the YMCA; she has also done fund-raising for Arena Stage, the Kennedy Center and the Martha's Vineyard Hospital.

CHUNKY GUACAMOLE

This can be served either with a chili, as a dip with tostados or as a salad.

Serves: 8-10

INGREDIENTS

4 ripe avocado pears
3 tbsps lemon or lime juice
1 large tomato, diced or minced
1-2 cloves garlic, grated
6 diced green onions (optional)
1 tsp Worcestershire sauce
A few drops Tabasco, or other hot sauce
Salt and pepper to taste

METHOD

Mash two of the avocados thoroughly with a fork. Chop the other two into dime-sized chunks. Combine all the ingredients and mix well. Adjust the citrus juice and salt to taste.

The texture and seasoning of a guacamole are very much according to personal taste. It may be very smooth and quite bland or chunky and hot and spicy. We prefer the latter. As a salad, the guacamole looks best served on a bed of lettuce and garnished with a criss-cross pattern of red pepper strips.

FRANK IKARD'S CHILI

Chili is a favorite dish of most Texans. However, they can never agree on the best way to prepare it. As a result, most recipes for chili are the same, yet each is different. Everyone makes chili using the same ingredients, but in their own special proportions.

Serves: 6-8

INGREDIENTS

3lbs very coarse ground lean beef (chuck or round)
1 cup chopped onions
2 cloves garlic, minced
4 tbsps ground chili peppers or chili powder
1 tbsp cumin
1 tbsp oregano
1 8oz can tomatoes in juice
1 tbsp red pepper
1 tbsp paprika
Salt to taste
2 cups water
2 tbsps masa flour (Mexican cornmeal), or regular flour

METHOD

Sear the meat in a heavy iron skillet, breaking it up with a fork as it browns. Once browned, remove the meat to a large pot and add the onion, garlic, chili pepper, cumin, oregano, tomatoes, red pepper, paprika, salt and water. Cook over a low heat for 1 hour or until the meat is tender. Mix the flour with 2 tbsps water to make a paste and add to the pan. Cook for a further 20-30 minutes, until thick. If the chili is too dry and thick, add 1 cup water or coffee.

The chili is best prepared the day before serving. If it is refrigerated overnight, the fat rises to the top and easily be removed before the chili is reheated.

JALAPENO CORNBREAD

Makes: 1 large loaf

INGREDIENTS

3 eggs, beaten
1½ cups sweet milk
2 tsps sugar
½ cup vegetable or corn oil
1 large onion

Above: Frank Ikard's Chili, Jalapeno Cornbread and Chunky Guacamole.

1 1/2 cups grated extra sharp Cheddar cheese
3 cups cornmeal
(yellow cornbread mix can be substituted)
1 tsp baking powder
12oz pickled jalapeno peppers

METHOD

Add all the ingredients to a blender bowl and purée. If your blender is not large enough to hold everything, leave out the cheese and half the cornmeal. Purée the remaining ingredients, then turn the blender contents into a large mixing bowl. Add the cheese and cornmeal and stir vigorously about 1 minute.

If the mixture seems thin, add more cornmeal until the texture resembles regular cornbread. A too thin mixture means the cooked cornbread will be sticky. Pour the mixture into a greased loaf or muffin pan and bake in a preheated 400° oven 40-45 minutes for a loaf, or 25-30 minutes for muffins, or until brown on top.

To make the cornbread hotter, substitute jalapeno pickle juice for part of the milk. To make it milder, reduce the amount of jalapenos.

JALAPENO RELISH

INGREDIENTS

2 gallons green tomatoes, coarsely chopped
(4 medium tomatoes = 1 quart, approximately)
8 onions, coarsely chopped
1 quart jalapeno peppers
6 cups sugar

½ cup salt
2 tbsps black pepper
½ gallon white vinegar

METHOD

Place all the vegetables in a large pan. In a separate bowl, combine the sugar, salt, pepper and vinegar and stir until thoroughly mixed. Pour the liquid over the vegetables and bring to a boil.

After the mixture has simmered about 10 minutes, turn off the heat. Spoon the relish into prepared canning jars and seal. Let the relish sit at least 1 month before serving.

OLD-FASHIONED CHICKEN STEW WITH DUMPLINGS

I make this over two days, cooking the chicken the first day, refrigerating, and then skimming the fat off.

Serves: 4

INGREDIENTS

1 stewing chicken, cut into portions
Carrots
1 large onion
Celery
3 bay leaves
Salt
Peppercorns
20 pearl onions
3 tbsps butter
3 tbsps flour

Dumplings

2 cups flour, unsifted
1 tbsp baking powder
1 tbsp salt
1 tbsp thyme
1½ cups heavy cream

METHOD

Put the chicken in a large pot together with 1 carrot, the onion, 1 stalk of celery, 3 bay leaves, salt and peppercorns. Add enough water to make 3 cups of stock, once the chicken is cooked. Stew gently for 1½ hours. After this

Right: Old Fashioned Chicken Stew with Dumplings.

time, skin and bone the chicken, if desired and return to the pan. Remove the carrot, onion and celery. Strain off 3 cups of stock. Add the pearl onions and extra chopped celery and carrot to the chicken.

Mix the stock with the 3 tbsps butter and 3 tbsps flour over a low heat until smooth and slightly thickened, then pour back over the chicken. Season to taste.

Make the dumpling by mixing together all the dry ingredients and then quickly stirring in the cream, using a fork. The mixture should be moist and sticky. Drop the dumplings by teaspoonfuls into the stew and allow to cook at a simmer for 10 minutes, covered, followed by a further 10 minutes, uncovered.

CARMEN'S BLACK BEANS WITH RICE

Serves: 4

INGREDIENTS

16oz black beans (turtle beans)
4 pork chops
1 tbsp Wesson oil
2 strips of bacon
1 clove garlic, minced
1 medium-sized onion, chopped

METHOD

Soak the beans overnight in water to cover. Drain and discard any unwanted particles.

Cook the pork chops in a skillet. Remove any bones or fat.

In a large pan, heat the oil over a medium heat. Chop the bacon and brown quickly in the oil. Add the garlic and onions and cook until lightly browned. Add the beans to the pan and cover with water. Bring the beans to a boil, reduce the heat and cover the pan. Allow the beans to cook, checking the water from time to time and topping up with hot water, if necessary. Cut up the pork chops and add to the beans, bringing back to a boil. Cook for 1½ to 2 hours, in total.

Serve over fluffy white rice. Top with chopped white onion and drizzle over olive oil and white vinegar to taste.

Facing page: Carmen's Black Beans with Rice.

CHILI BEANS

Some people insist that beans be served with chili. Sometimes they are mixed in with the chili. However, if served, we prefer them on the side. Beans here mean dried beans, usually pinto beans, although red beans (not kidney beans) could also be used.

Serves: 6

INGREDIENTS

1lb dried pinto beans
1 large onion, chopped
2 cloves garlic, minced
1 tbsp cumin
3 tbsps chili powder
2 tbsps bacon drippings
Salt and pepper to taste

METHOD

Pick over the beans carefully, then soak overnight in enough water to cover. Next day, rinse the beans. Put the beans in a pot and cover with water. Mix in the onion, garlic, cumin, chili powder, bacon drippings and salt and pepper to taste. Cook over a low heat until the beans are tender. If the water cooks away, add more. The longer the beans cook the better.

This dish can either be mixed into a chili or served as a side dish.

BEEF STEW WITH FRENCH BREAD

This stew should be served with a little green salad and a small loaf of French bread per person. To drink, red wine makes the best accompaniment.

Serves: 8

INGREDIENTS

4lbs beef, cut into 1-inch cubes
Flour
Butter
Oil
2 quarts boiling water
3 6 fl oz cans V8 juice

2lbs small red potatoes, peeled
1lb carrots, scraped and cut
2lbs turnips, peeled and cut into large cubes
1½ lbs pearl onions, peeled
1 cup red wine
Salt and pepper
Parsley to taste

METHOD

Put the beef into a ziploc bag with enough flour to coat and shake together. Sauté the beef in a little butter and oil until it is brown. Transfer the browned meat to a large pot, then cover with 2 quarts boiling water to seal the juices in the meat. Add the V8 juice. Cover the pot and simmer for 1 hour either on top of the stove or in a preheated 325° oven.

Add the vegetables, 1 cup of red wine, or more, and salt and pepper to taste and cook until the vegetables are tender. Garnish with chopped parsley. The gravy can be thinned with more water if desired, to give more juices for dipping the French bread.

CREAM PUDDING WITH ICED ORANGES

Serves: 8

INGREDIENTS

1 cup sugar
1 envelope unflavored gelatin
2¼ cups heavy cream
2 cups plain yogurt or sour cream
1 tsp vanilla extract
8 seedless oranges
2 tbsps sugar

METHOD

In a saucepan, mix the 1 cup sugar with the gelatin. Stir in the cream and allow the mixture to stand for 5 minutes. Heat gently for a few minutes, stirring, until the sugar and gelatin have completely dissolved. Chill for about 1 hour,

Beef Stew with French Bread.

until slightly thickened. Fold in the yogurt or sour cream and the vanilla extract. Chill for several hours. It will set somewhat like a soft pudding.

Prepare the oranges. Cut a slice from the top of each orange. Using a serrated knife, cut off the peel in spiral fashion, cutting deeply enough to remove all the white pith. Do this over a bowl to catch the juices. Cut along each dividing membrane from the outside to the core and remove the orange segments, one by one. When all the oranges have been segmented, add the 2 tbsps sugar. Allow to stand for 10 minutes, then pour off the juice that will have collected. Measure and add enough extra juice to make up 1 cup. Cover the orange segments and refrigerate. Pour the juice into a freezing tray, and freeze.

To serve, arrange the orange segments in a bowl and top first with the cream pudding and then with shavings of the frozen juice.

MARINATED ORANGE SLICES

This makes a simple and delicious dessert
to follow a chili supper.

INGREDIENTS

1 large eating orange per guest
(blood oranges are the most beautiful)
Sugar to taste
Grated lemon rind and lemon juice
(1 lemon for every 5 oranges)
Maraschino cherry liqueur, Grand Marnier or Kirsch
(2-3 tbsps for every 5 oranges)

METHOD

Peel the oranges, removing as much of the membrane as possible. Slice them in rounds, as thickly as possible. Lay the slices in a dish and sprinkle with sugar to taste and then with a little grated lemon rind. Pour over the lemon juice; the aim is to coat the oranges, but not to make juice - the sugar and the oranges will already have made some. Cover with plastic wrap and refrigerate overnight, turning once.

Before serving, add the liqueur to the oranges. Arrange 3-5 slices on a dessert plate, pour over a little of the juices, and garnish with fresh mint.

Left: Cream Pudding with Iced Oranges, and Marinated Orange Slices.

Seated as if in judgement, the colossal statue of "Honest Abe," designed by Daniel Chester French, surveys the Washington Monument and Capitol from its vantage point in the Lincoln Memorial.

·Mrs. Raymond Howar·

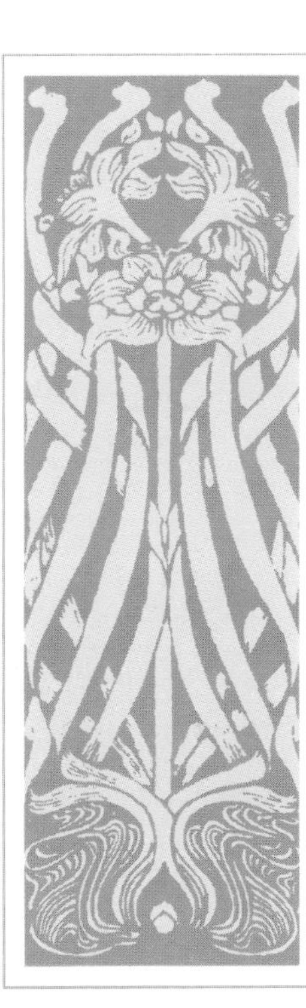

"If I could exist on desserts alone, I would," admits Pam Howar. A bountiful dessert table is a trademark of her personal style of entertaining; it is imaginative, beautifully arranged, and overflows, she says, "with all the things that lighten and gladden the heart." Pam and her husband Ray, a real estate investor, cultivate their favorite orchids in a greenhouse adjacent to their Georgian-style home, and orchids appear in profusion throughout the house most of the year. Pam's favorite party is a family reception at Christmas because it gives families an opportunity to be together and children, including the Howars' young daughter Elizabeth, an occasion for putting on their best party clothes. Five years ago Pam co-founded the Parents' Music Resource Center with Tipper Gore, wife of the Tennessee senator, Susan Baker, wife of the secretary of state, and Sally Nevius. Concerned with educating parents about the lyrics in the music their children hear, the Center has drawn national media attention. Pam is also involved in many of Washington's charitable organizations, including the Entertaining People event for the Washington Home, the Child Health Center Board of Children's Hospital, the Jamestown Foundation, the Alexander Graham Bell Association for the Deaf, the Symphony Ball and the Washington Antiques Show.

Pam's Cheese Tart

Makes: 1 9-inch tart

Method

Make a regular shortcrust pastry, adding 2 tbsps of Parmesan cheese. Use to line a 9-inch pie dish. Slice pap-cooked apples over the bottom of the pie shell. Cover with crumbled cheure (chopped parsley and Brie cubes). Repeat the layers.

Bake the tart for 40 minutes in a preheated 350° oven until the pastry is cooked and golden brown. Serve with French bread.

Apple and Pear Cheese Cookies

Ingredients

1 lb unsalted butter
1 lb flour
1 lb Parmesan cheese
1/2 tsp cayenne pepper
1/2 cup walnuts
3 Granny Smith apples
3 pears
1 tbsp butter

A bountiful dessert table, beautifully arranged, is a trademark of Pam Howar's style of entertaining.

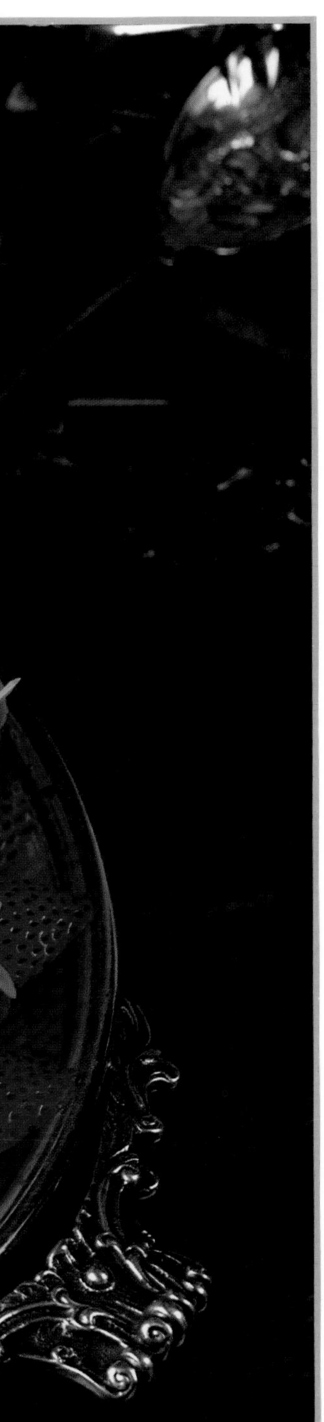

Desserts should "lighten and gladden the heart" according to Pam Howar, and that is exactly the effect of this strawberry and cream creation (left).

METHOD

In a blender, blend the 1lb butter, the flour, cheese and cayenne pepper. Add the nuts. Form the mixture into long rolls and chill. Sliver the apples and pears. Sauté them quickly in the 1 tbsp butter in a frying pan. Slice the rolls into cookies and place on cookie sheets. Top with the apples and pears. Bake in a preheated 425° oven for 3-5 minutes.

CHOCOLATE MACADAMIA NUT TOFFEES

INGREDIENTS

1 stick of unsalted butter
8oz dark brown sugar
3oz dark chocolate
1 large jar macadamia nuts

METHOD

In a saucepan, melt the butter with the sugar over a low heat. Add the chocolate, melt and allow to bubble for 2 minutes. Add the nuts and mix in well. Spoon out the mixture onto an oiled baking sheet and leave to cool.

VANILLA CHERRY ICE IN CHOCOLATE MERINGUE NESTS

Serves: 10

INGREDIENTS

4 egg whites
8oz fine sugar
2 tbsps chocolate chips
1 pint vanilla ice cream
½ lb fresh cherries, pitted
4 tbsps cherry liqueur

METHOD

Whip the egg whites stiffly. Fold in the sugar and chocolate chips. Pipe the meringue into nests on an oiled baking sheet. Bake in a preheated 150° oven for 6 hours.

Remove the nests from the oven and allow to cool. Mash the ice cream with the cherries and the liqueur. Fill the nests with the ice and serve immediately.

CHOCOLATE LEAF CAKE

Makes: 1 9-inch cake

INGREDIENTS

2oz unsalted butter
4oz plain chocolate
3 eggs, separated
2oz fine sugar
1 tbsp flour
2oz ground almonds
1 tsp vanilla extract
6oz plain chocolate
2 sticks butter
12oz chocolate chips

METHOD

Beat the 2oz butter in a bowl. Soften the 4oz chocolate and beat into the butter. Add the egg yolks one at a time. Fold in the sugar, flour, almonds and vanilla extract, mixing well. Beat the egg whites and fold in gently. Pour the batter into a buttered cake pan. Bake for 45 minutes in a preheated 350° oven. Turn out and allow to cool completely.

Melt the 6oz plain chocolate with the 2 sticks butter over a low heat. Slice the cake horizontally into 3 even layers. Sandwich the layers together again with the chocolate / butter mixture, reserving some to spread over the top and sides of the cake. Melt the chocolate chips gently over a low heat. Spread thinly onto wax paper. When completely cold, peel the paper away. Use these chocolate sheets to cover the finished cake.

ORANGE PUFFS

Serves: 8-10

INGREDIENTS

Pâte à Choux

1 cup water
2oz butter
4oz flour
4 eggs
1 tsp sugar

Right: Chocolate Leaf Cake.

Hand-made chocolates, set within a box created from chocolate and marzipan, show how much imagination goes into the desserts and confectionery offered by Pam Howar.

Filling

1 pint heavy cream
1 envelope gelatin
1 cup fresh orange juice

METHOD

To make the choux pastry, boil the water with the butter. Stir in the flour and cook the mixture for 1 minute. Beat in the eggs one at a time and then add the sugar. Pipe the choux pastry into rounds on an oiled baking sheet and cook for 7-10 minutes in a preheated 425° oven. Lower the oven temperature to 350° and allow the choux balls to dry out. Remove from the oven and leave to cool.

When the choux balls are completely cold, whip the cream. Dissolve the gelatin in the orange juice and allow to gel. Fold the cream and the juice together. Refrigerate for one hour. Fill the choux balls with the orange cream and pile them into a pyramid shape. Decorate the pyramid with either spun sugar or grated orange rind.

Mrs Raymond Howard

Mocha Mousse with Raspberry Cream

Serves: 12

Ingredients

8 large eggs
$^{1}/_{2}$ cup sugar
8oz good dark chocolate, melted over a low heat
1 envelope of gelatin, dissolved in 2 tbsps strong black coffee
1 pint heavy cream
2 tbsps Kaluha
2 pints fresh raspberries
$^{2}/_{3}$ pint heavy cream, whipped with 2 tbsps sugar and 1 tsp vanilla extract
18 chocolate coffee beans, to decorate

Method

Separate the eggs. Whip the yolks with the sugar until light. Add the melted chocolate and the coffee / gelatin mixture. Whip the 1 pint heavy cream and fold into the egg yolk mixture. Stir in the Kaluha. Whip the egg whites and fold into the mousse.

Pour one third of the mousse into a soufflé dish. Reserve some raspberries for decoration and spoon half of those remaining over the mousse. Dot with whipped cream. Repeat the layers and finish with the final third of the mousse. Decorate with the reserved raspberries and the chocolate coffee beans before serving.

The marble splendor of the Main Reading Room of the Library of Congress.

· Mrs. John Chapoton ·

Sally Chapoton often prepares food with a Southwestern flavor and it comes naturally because she and her attorney husband John have strong Texas-Bush connections. The Chapotons moved here from Houston in 1969 when he was named Tax Legislative Counsel of the Treasury. After a few years back home again, they returned in 1981 when he was appointed Assistant Secretary of the Treasury and have been in the Capital ever since. Sally was a Bush for Congress volunteer in 1966 and 1968, a volunteer for Bush Headquarters in 1988, and chaired the nine Inaugural Balls in 1989. Her Southwestern recipes are happy surprises, like crabmeat with flour tortillas and guacamole and sour cream on top. A favorite summer weekend custom is a standing invitation to lunch by the pool for the Chapoton's college- and law school-age daughter and son and their friends. Since the party is open-ended, Sally serves an alfresco cold lunch, "a kind of movable feast." Aside from her involvement with several community organizations such as the Corcoran Gallery of Art, she is First Regent of the national board of Gunston Hall, a Virginia state-owned museum house, and recently chaired a benefit in Washington for the American Association of Royal Academy of Arts Trust, planning the two-day event and acquiring funding for it.

GUACAMOLE

Serves: 6-8

INGREDIENTS

3 avocados, mashed and seeds reserved
1 tomato, seeded and chopped
1 tbsp minced onion
1 tbsp cilantro or powdered coriander
2 tbsps lemon juice
3 slices pickled jalapeno peppers, chopped
Salt and pepper to taste

METHOD

Combine all the ingredients, mixing together well. Add the reserved seeds to the mixture and cover. The seeds will help retain the green color of the avocados.

SHRIMP AND SCALLOP CEVICHE

Serves: 6-8

INGREDIENTS

1lb scallops
1lb shrimp
6 fresh limes or 1 cup lime juice
1/4 cup chopped cilantro or parsley
1/2 cup olive oil
1 small onion, chopped
6 slices pickled jalapeno peppers, chopped
3 tomatoes

METHOD

Cut the scallops and shrimp into bite-sized pieces. Add all the remaining ingredients except the tomatoes. Cover and refrigerate for 12 hours. One hour before serving, add the tomatoes, chopped and seeded. Serve the dish with a dollop of curried mayonnaise on top.

GREEN MAYONNAISE

Makes: 1 cup

INGREDIENTS

1/2 cup fresh spinach, minced
1/2 cup fresh watercress leaves, minced
1/2 cup fresh tarragon leaves, minced
1/2 tsp lemon
1 cup mayonnaise

METHOD

Place the first three ingredients in a sieve. Pour boiling water over the leaves to wilt them, then leave to drain thoroughly. Combine all the ingredients, mixing well.

GRILLED CHICKEN BREASTS

Serves: 4

INGREDIENTS

4 whole boneless chicken breasts
3/4 cup olive oil
1/2 cup soy sauce
1/4 cup Worcestershire sauce

Facing page: Guacamole, Marinated Mixed Peppers, Shrimp and Scallop Ceviche, and Grilled Chicken Breasts arranged around a Russian Salad – Sally Chapoton's alfresco lunches are a feast of Southwestern-style cooking.

Mrs. John Chapoton

Above: tangy quartered pineapple, garnished with melon, strawberries and blueberries, is a delicious and refreshing end to a satisfying meal – it goes well with cheese, too.

Fresh Vegetable Sauce

1 tomato, chopped
1 green pepper, chopped
¼ cup onion, chopped
½ cup olive oil

METHOD

Marinate the chicken breasts in the ¾ cup olive oil, the soy sauce and Worcestershire sauce for 30 minutes. Remove the breasts from the marinade and cook on a hot grill for 10 minutes. Turn and cook another 10 minutes.

To make the sauce, place the chopped vegetables in a bowl and toss with the olive oil. Serve the chicken breasts with either this sauce or green mayonnaise.

MARINATED MIXED PEPPERS

Serves: 4

INGREDIENTS

3 red peppers
3 yellow peppers
½ cup olive oil
1 lemon
1 clove garlic, chopped
¼ cup fresh basil, chopped

METHOD

Roast the peppers on a cookie sheet for 20 minutes in a preheated 400° oven. Turn the peppers and roast for a further 20 minutes. Remove from the oven and cover the peppers for 15 minutes. Peel the peppers, seed and slice into equal-sized strips. Place these in a bowl and toss with the oil. Add the garlic and basil and mix together gently.

RUSSIAN SALAD

Serves: 12

INGREDIENTS

2 cups cooked cubed potatoes (small cubes)
2 cups cooked cubed carrots
2 cups cubed celery
2 cups cooked cubed beets
2 cups cooked green peas
3/4 cup olive oil
1/4 cup wine vinegar
1 clove garlic, minced
1/8 tsp salt
Pepper to taste
Mayonnaise

METHOD

In a bowl combine the cubed vegetables and the peas. Add the oil, vinegar, garlic, salt and pepper. Mix and leave to stand for 1 hour. Before serving, stir in enough mayonnaise to bind the mixture.

LIME MOUSSE

Serves: 4

INGREDIENTS

4 egg yolks
1/2 cup sugar
1/2 cup fresh lime juice
1/4 tsp salt
1-1 1/2 cups heavy cream
1 tsp grated lime peel

METHOD

Beat the egg yolks until foamy. Thoroughly mix in the sugar, lime juice and salt. Cook this mixture in a double boiler until the sauce thickens. Set aside to cool. In a separate bowl, beat the cream until stiff. Fold in the cooled sauce and add the lime peel. Place the mousse in a mold which has been rinsed in cold water and chilled. Chill until ready to serve.

Unmold onto a serving plate and decorate with thin slices of fresh lime.

Lime Mousse.

A kaleidoscope of color in springtime Washington.

· Washington Hostess Cookbook ·

· MRS. MARVIN LEATH ·

Alta Leath came to Washington with her husband Marvin when he was elected as a Democrat to the House from Waco, Texas, in 1978. She disputes the clichés about the city being competitive. "I find everybody can do their own thing and it's acceptable. It's not always the finest and grandest." She gets support and encouragement from the Congressional Wives Club and Congressional Wives Fellowship Group. Oriental art, she says, taught her balance, proportion, rhythm and harmony – the design elements she follows in her home and business. The Leaths' house is a restful haven decorated in happy colors like apricot. Her business is the Altomar Collection, a shop selling hand-crafted, one-of-a-kind jewelry in the Watergate Hotel and a branch in Dallas. Alta's hobby, and "therapy," is growing plants; she trains topiaries of herbs, eugenias and ivy and uses them with a tureen or Lalique crystal and Steuben glass animals to create effortless centerpieces. She has over 200 plants, including orchids. Alta is practical about desserts. "I love homemade desserts and won't waste calories and cholesterol unless they're really wonderful!" Most of her desserts are based on old family recipes, but like all confident cooks, she experiments a lot and adds her own touches.

COFFEE ANGEL FOOD CAKE

Makes: 1 10-inch cake

INGREDIENTS

1½ cups sifted sugar
1 cup sifted cake flour
½ tsp salt
1¼ cups egg whites (10-12)
1¼ tsps cream of tartar
1 tsp vanilla extract
1 tbsp instant coffee powder

Butter Icing

½ cup butter
¼ tsp salt
2½ cups sifted confectioners' sugar
2 tbsps instant coffee powder, dissolved in 3 tbsps water
2 tsps vanilla extract

METHOD

Add ½ cup of the sugar to the flour. Sift together 4 times. Add the salt to the egg whites and beat with a flat wire whisk or rotary egg beater until foamy. Sprinkle the cream of tartar over the egg whites and continue beating to the soft peak stage. Take ¼ cup of the mixture and put in the coffee to dissolve. Add the remaining cup of sugar by sprinkling it ¼ cup at a time over the egg whites and

From left: Mint Dressing for Fresh Fruit, Ice Cream Dessert Mold, Coffee Angel Food Cake, Apricot Roll, Pineapple Sponge Layer Cake, Banana Pudding with Raspberry Sauce, and Chocolate Mousse Cake.

Verner

Facing page: Chocolate Mousse Cake.
Above: Coffee Angel Food Cake.

blending it in carefully. Fold in the flavorings. Sift the flour and sugar mixture over the egg whites a quarter at a time and fold in quickly and lightly. Pour the mixture into an ungreased round 10-inch tube pan. Bake in a preheated 350° oven for 35-45 minutes. Remove the cake from the oven and invert the pan on a cooling rack.

For the butter icing, cream the butter and then add the salt and sugar gradually, beating continuously. Add the dissolved coffee and the vanilla extract and beat the mixture until light and fluffy. Use to decorate the cooled cake.

CHOCOLATE MOUSSE CAKE

Makes: 1 8-inch-square cake

INGREDIENTS

5 egg whites
Pinch cream of tartar
3/4 cup sugar
1 3/4 cups confectioners' sugar
1/3 cup unsweetened cocoa
13oz semisweet chocolate
7 egg whites

¼ tsp cream of tartar
3 cups heavy cream
1½ tsps vanilla extract

METHOD

In a large bowl beat the 5 egg whites with the pinch cream of tartar to the soft peak stage. Beat in the sugar, 2 tbsps at a time, and continue to beat until it holds stiff peaks. Sift the confectioners' sugar with the cocoa and fold into the meringue mixture. Using an inverted 8-inch-square pan as a guide, trace 3 squares on sheets of parchment paper. Place these on baking sheets. Divide the meringue between the squares, spreading it evenly to the edges. Bake in a preheated 300° oven for 1¼ hours, alternating the sheets for even baking. Transfer the meringue layers to racks, cool and peel off the paper.

Melt the chocolate in a double boiler, then cool to lukewarm. Beat the 7 egg whites with the ¼ tsp cream of tartar to the stiff peak stage. In another bowl beat the chilled cream with the vanilla extract to the stiff peak stage. Fold the chocolate into the egg whites and then fold in the cream.

To assemble the cake, put 1 meringue layer on a cake stand and spread thickly with chocolate mousse. Repeat with the remaining meringue layers and mousse, saving a little mousse to pipe decoratively over the finished cake. Chill for at least 4 hours, or overnight.

MINT DRESSING FOR FRESH FRUIT

Makes: about 2½ cups

INGREDIENTS

¾ cup sugar
1 tsp dry mustard
1 tsp salt
⅓ cup apple cider vinegar
2 tbsps chopped onion
3 tbsps fresh mint leaves
1 cup Wesson oil

METHOD

Mix the sugar, mustard, salt and vinegar in a blender. Add the onion and mint and blend on high speed. Add the oil very slowly, blending until thick. Store this dressing in the refrigerator and serve it on fresh fruit.

Right: Mint Dressing for Fresh Fruit.

PINEAPPLE SPONGE LAYER CAKE

Makes: 1 9-inch layer cake

INGREDIENTS

11 egg yolks
2 cups sugar
1 cup milk, heated
2½ cups (less 1 tbsp) cake flour
2 tsps baking powder
¼ tsp salt
1 tsp vanilla extract
½ cup melted butter

Filling

1½ cups sugar
2 tbsps flour (heaping)
Pinch salt
Grated rind from 1 orange
1 No.2 can crushed pineapple

METHOD

Beat the egg yolks until light and lemon colored. Add the sugar and beat. Sift the flour with the baking powder and salt and add alternately with the milk to the egg yolks and sugar mixture. Mix in the vanilla extract. Fold in the melted butter, mixing well.

Pour the cake mixture into three greased and floured 9-inch cake pans and bake in a preheated 350° oven for 30-35 minutes.

To make the filling mix together all the ingredients in a saucepan and cook over a gentle heat, stirring continuously, until thick.

Assemble by sandwiching together the cooled cake layers with some of the filling and spreading the rest over the top and around the sides. The cake can be iced with 7 minute frosting, if desired.

BANANA PUDDING WITH RASPBERRY SAUCE

Serves: 4

Pineapple Sponge Layer Cake.

INGREDIENTS

1½ cups sugar
4½ tbsps flour
3 cups milk
2 tbsps butter
¼ tsp salt
4 eggs, separated
3 tsps vanilla extract
12-16oz frozen raspberries
¼ cup sugar
1 tbsp cornstarch, mixed to a paste with a little water
Vanilla wafers
3-4 large bananas, sliced

METHOD

Place 1¼ cups of the sugar, the flour, milk, butter and salt in a double boiler and cook, stirring constantly, over a gentle heat. When the mixture begins to thicken, mix a small amount of this custard with the beaten egg yolks and vanilla extract, then return this to the double boiler and continue to cook until the mixture thickens. Beat the egg whites with the remaining ¼ cup sugar until stiff. Fold the custard into the beaten egg whites.

Defrost the raspberries and push through a sieve to remove the seeds. Place the resultant purée in a pan with the ¼ cup sugar and bring to a boil. Boil about 3 minutes to make a syrup and thicken with the cornstarch paste.

In a crystal compote, layer the vanilla wafers, sliced bananas, then the custard with raspberry sauce spooned around its edge. End with a layer of custard with raspberry sauce on top.

ICE CREAM DESSERT IN MOLD

Serves: 8-10

INGREDIENTS

1 cup grated semisweet or bittersweet chocolate
2 cups finely chopped nuts
1 gallon vanilla ice cream, softened
2 tsps vanilla extract (optional)
Orange, lime and raspberry sherbets

METHOD

Mix the chocolate and nuts with the softened ice cream

Right: Ice Cream Dessert Mold.

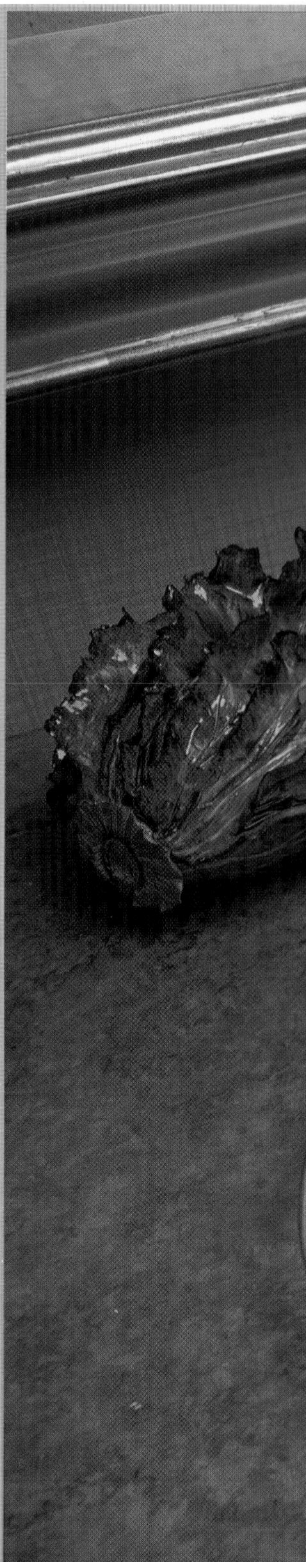

and the vanilla extract, if using. Put half this mixture in an angel cake tube pan. Make balls from the orange, lime and raspberry sherbets and arrange a double layer of these over the ice cream. Cover with the remaining ice cream. Put in the freezer.

When ready to serve, unmold by placing on a serving plate and covering with a warm wet cloth to loosen the mold, so it can be slipped off easily. After unmolding, cover the dessert with whipped cream, which has been sweetened to taste, flavored with 1 tsp vanilla extract and tinted pink with a little cake coloring.

After covering with whipped cream, the dessert can be returned to the freezer until required. It should be left at room temperature for 20 minutes before serving to soften slightly.

APRICOT ROLL

Makes: 4 rolls

INGREDIENTS

Cream Cheese Pastry (make 24 hours ahead)

8oz cream cheese
2 sticks butter
2 cups flour

Filling

2 cups apricot preserves
1 can shredded coconut
1 cup chopped pecans

1 cup raisins
1 tbsp lemon juice
1 tbsp grated lemon rind
1 tbsp orange juice
1 tbsp grated orange rind
Rum butter (melt butter and add rum to taste)
Powdered sugar

METHOD

Blend the cream cheese and butter together in a processor or with a pastry blender. Add the flour and work together until a ball of pastry is obtained. Refrigerate. Take the pastry out and leave at room temperature 30 minutes before using.

Preheat the oven to 450°. Combine all the remaining ingredients except the rum butter and powdered sugar.

Divide the pastry into four and roll out each quarter into an oblong shape. Spread each oblong with one quarter of the filling mixture. Roll up like a jelly roll and place on a baking sheet. Brush with rum butter, or simply with melted butter if preferred. Bake in the preheated oven for 15 minutes, then reduce the heat to 350° and continue baking for 1 hour. Slice while still hot and serve sprinkled with powdered sugar.

Facing page: Banana Pudding with Raspberry Sauce.
Above: Apricot Roll.

The pediment and dome of the Capitol.

· MRS. RINALDO PETRIGNANI ·

Anne Merete, wife of the Italian Ambassador Rinaldo Petrignani, welcomes between eight and ten thousand guests a year to Villa Firenze, the Ambassador's residence. The Tudor-style country house, set in a 22-acre park in the middle of Washington, is ideal for entertaining, with a charming gazebo decorated by Italian architect Piero Pinta, broad terraces, and Fortuny- and Ratti-draped reception rooms with Venetian glass chandeliers. The Ambassador, a career diplomat, was previously posted in Brussels and Geneva. "Italian Food," says Mrs. Petrignani, "is based on variety, freshness of products, the quality of the ingredients and the aesthetic pleasure that comes from a natural presentation." She finds Washington delightful and very interesting since a wife participates to a larger extent than in some European communities. She is a member of Number One International Neighbors Club, a mixture of women from residential, congressional and official Washington, the Women's Committee of the Corcoran Gallery of Art, Board member of the School of Languages and Linguistics, Georgetown University, National Rehabilitation Hospital Board of Associates.

FAGIOLI AL FORNO CON SALVIA

Serves: 6-8

INGREDIENTS

1lb Great Northern white beans
½ cup olive oil
4 cloves garlic
2 cups tomatoes, peeled
1 bunch fresh sage leaves
Salt and pepper, to taste

METHOD

Soak the beans overnight. The next day simmer the beans in water for about two hours, or until they are tender. Drain the beans and set aside.

In a skillet sauté the tomatoes and the garlic. Add the fresh sage leaves. Toss the beans with the tomato, garlic, and sage mixture and turn into a large baking dish. Bake, covered, for 1½ hours.

ROTOLO DI VITELLO CON UOVA E SPINACI

Serves: 6-8

INGREDIENTS

4 eggs
1lb cooked fresh spinach
2lbs leg of veal, sliced
½ cup butter
8 Italian pancetta, or bacon
¼ cup pine nuts

Right: Fagioli al Forno con Salvia, and Rotolo di Vitello con Uova e Spinaci.

4 tbsps olive oil
1 cup beef stock
Parsley, to garnish
Salt and pepper, to taste

METHOD

Beat the eggs and fry them as you would an omelette. Set aside. Sauté the cooked spinach. Pound the veal to make it thinner. Spread the egg omelette over the veal, layer the bacon on top and sprinkle with the pine nuts. Top with the spinach

Roll the veal with the stuffing like a jelly roll and tie it securely with a string. Sauté the veal roll, until browned on all sides. Add the beef stock and season to taste. Simmer for 1½ hours, or until tender. When done, remove the string and cut the veal roll into slices. Serve hot with parsley garnishing.

Above: Pomodori Ripieni con Riso.

POMODORI RIPIENI CON RISO

Serves: 6

INGREDIENTS

6 large tomatoes
1½ cups cooked rice
3 tbsps olive oil

3 tbsps chopped fresh parsley
12 large basil leaves
Salt and pepper, to taste

METHOD

Slice the tops off the tomatoes, remove the inside pulp and set aside. Put a little salt and sugar inside each tomato and turn upside down to drain. Mix the rice, oil, parsley and the remaining tomato pulp. Let this mixture marinate for one hour.

Stuff the tomatoes first with a large basil leaf, then fill with the reserved rice mixture, topping with another basil leaf. Cover with the tops. Arrange the tomatoes in a baking dish. Sprinkle with olive oil. Bake for an hour at 375°.

Facing page: Pasta con Melanzane. Above: Insalata di Peperoni Arrosto.

PASTA CON MELANZANE

Serves: 6-8

INGREDIENTS

½ lb sliced eggplant
3 tbsps olive oil
1lb "penne rigate" (pen pasta with ridges)
½ lb pear-shaped tomatoes, peeled and chopped
10 basil leaves

2 tbsps Parmesan cheese
Salt and pepper, to taste

METHOD

Slice the eggplant thinly, sprinkle with salt, put in a colander and let it drain for two hours. Sauté the eggplant in the olive oil and set aside. Sauté the tomatoes and set aside.

Boil 4 quarts of water. When it boils, throw the penne in and cook for about 9 minutes until "al dente". When the pasta is done, drain well and mix it with the tomatoes, eggplant and fresh basil. Mix lightly for a few minutes in a large skillet over low heat and sprinkle with Parmesan cheese just before serving.

PESCE ALLA GRIGLIA CON ROSMARINO

Serves: 6

INGREDIENTS

1- 1½ lbs Black Sea bass
2 tbsps fresh rosemary leaves
Salt and pepper, to taste

METHOD

Season the fish with salt, pepper and rosemary. Grill for 25 minutes, alternating about 10-15 minutes on each side. Serve with fresh rosemary branches, as garnish.

INSALATA DI PEPERONI ARROSTO

Serves: 6-8

INGREDIENTS

3 each: green, red and yellow bell peppers
4 cloves garlic, chopped
¼ cup chopped parsley
1 cup olive oil
1 lemon
Salt and pepper to taste

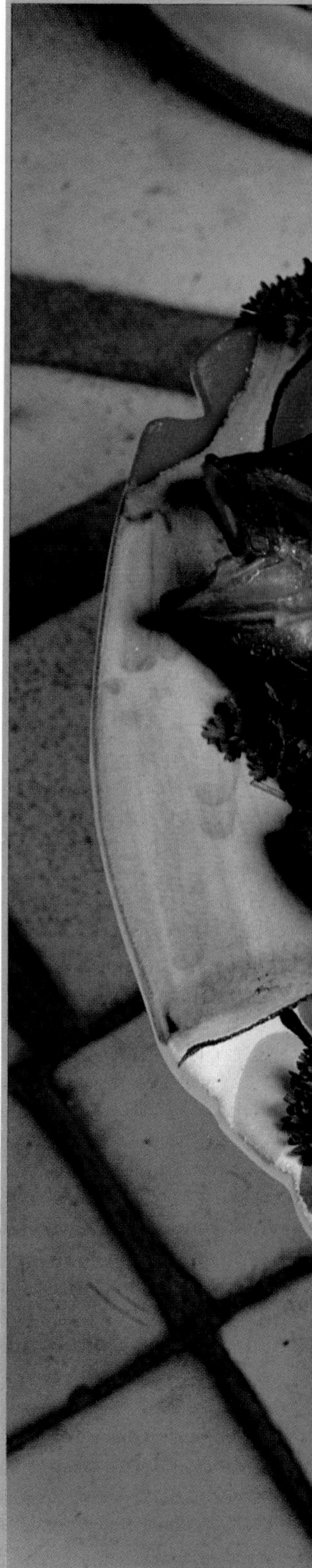

Right: Pesce alla Griglia con Rosmarino.

MONTRESOR
BIANCO DI CUSTOZA

METHOD

Roast the peppers, until cooked. Remove the seeds and peel. Cut them into thin strips. Mix the chopped garlic, parsley and peppers into a salad bowl, pour over the olive oil and lemon juice.

PESCHE AL VINO BIANCO

Serves: 6

INGREDIENTS

6 peaches
1 pint white wine
Mint leaves

METHOD

Peel the peaches and slice them thinly into wedges. Arrange the sliced peaches in champagne glasses and pour the wine over, to cover them. Decorate with mint leaves.
Note: this dessert should be prepared at the last minute since the peaches will darken if you let them stand too long.

"MOUSSE" AL CIOCCOLATO

Serves: 6-8

INGREDIENTS

9oz semisweet chocolate
8 tbsps melted butter
4 eggs, separated
$^{1}/_{4}$ cup sugar

METHOD

Melt the chocolate in a double boiler. Stir in the melted butter. Remove the chocolate from the heat and thoroughly stir in the egg yolks. Whip the egg whites until frothy, then add the sugar. Pour the mixture into a container and chill until set.

A mouthwatering selection of dishes to cater for all tastes: Rotolo di Vitello con Uova e Spinaci, Pasta con Melanzane, "Mousse" al Cioccolato, Pesce alla Griglia con Rosmarino, Fagioli al Forno con Salvia, Pesche al Vino Bianco, Pomodori Ripieni con Riso, and Insalata di Peperoni Arrosto.

· Washington Hostess Cookbook ·

·INDEX·

· Washington Hostess Cookbook ·

· Acknowledgements ·

The publishers would like to express their special thanks to all the Washington Hostesses who gave so unstintingly of their time throughout the preparation of this book. Without their generous help and considerable patience, this book would not have been possible.

Thanks are also due to Cissie Coy for assisting in the coordination of the project; Maggi Wimsett and Jennifer Crier Johnston of DOSSIER MAGAZINE for their advice and contacts; to One Washington Circle Hotel, Washington, D.C. for providing accommodation and to Jutta Whitfield for making us feel at home during our stay; to Elizabeth and the staff of Lisboa Associates Inc., Washington, D.C. for the unrestricted use of office facilities; to Dominique Leborgne for assisting photographer Neil Sutherland with the styling and for general help; to Jean-Louis Paladin and his assistant Catherine Grove; to Patrick Doyle of Bluewillow for the magnificent flower arrangements. Catering services: Maynard & David, Potomac, Maryland; Jetton's of Texas, Inc., Fort Worth, Texas; Ridgewell's, Bethesda, Maryland; Design Cuisine; and The American University Dining Services, Marriott Corporation.